JUROR NUMBER 8

PALMETTO
PUBLISHING
Charleston, SC
www.PalmettoPublishing.com

Copyright © 2024 by Connie E. Curry

All rights reserved

No portion of this book may be reproduced, stored in a retrieval system, or transmitted in any form by any means- electronic, mechanical, photocopy, recording, or other- except for brief quotations in printed reviews, without prior permission of the author.

Paperback ISBN: 9798822961395
eBook ISBN: 9798822961401

JUROR NUMBER 8
THE TRIAL OF MATHEAU L. MOORE

CONNIE E. CURRY

*In Memory of Emily Noble
Forage on.
To my husband who always supports
me in everything I do.
I write, I read, and he listens.
To Matt, our friend.*

ACKNOWLEDGEMENT

If I get the honor of living into my 90's, I hope my mind and wisdom are like Betty Stimmel's. I want to thank Betty, who is ninety-one, for always being one of my best cheerleaders when reading my stories. She read the rough copies of my book as I wrote page after page. I so appreciated her young, sharp eyes.

I want to thank my husband who was probably tired of hearing me ranting about this trial for months after it was over. I love to read my work aloud to him to get his opinion or see his reactions.

This was not one of my many humor stories that he loves, but he listened to me read these chapters and supported my work.

Thank you, my dear friend, "The other Connie"—Connie Stephenson.

Thank you, Matt. Your positive attitude is amazing after all you have had to deal with. Your courage through all this was remarkable. Your pockets are empty, but your soul is rich.

I think of my mom, who loved to write also and always supported my writing and my opinion. She is missed.

PROLOGUE

I have always loved to write non-fictions books. My love is humor stories, but what I experienced as Juror Number 8 was profound. I was compelled to put this experience into words. This story needed to be heard from a juror perspective.

I am an emotional and enthusiastic person in all I do. This experience weighed heavily on my emotions. My career was taking care of people to make them comfortable and to help save lives. I was proud to help save Matt's life and I was saddened by Emily's life.

Matheau Moore and Emily Noble were both victims. The tax dollars and time spent incarcerating Matt, with loss of freedom for a crime he did not commit, was saddening. The money he had to spend; the social media circus was ridiculous.

Just a day and a half after he had reported his wife missing, he was accused of murder. How could the police officers possibly know she was dead? Her body had not been found. She could have just left home for whatever reason to return home later. They did not know, but immediately Matt became the scapegoat. The sharks were brutal, and Matt was the victim.

The Westerville Police Department had tunnel vision and was relentless in wanting to arrest him. So much time was wasted when Emily's body was found close to her home but took months to find. Why didn't the Westerville detectives walk into the woods, just feet from the road? We, as jurors, went into the woods on day one to see the location and discuss the case.

The months spent with Emily's skeleton body being shipped to two places for the prosecuting team to hear what they hoped to hear was undeserving to Emily. The comments and harassment Matt received from his neighbors and around the world were so disgusting.

Small town talk for Westerville, and a city with very few crimes like this, made the gossip grow and grow.

Social media comments were so unfair. Some accused Matt of killing both his children. Certainly not true. He was accused of not helping to look for Emily. Not true. He was accused of being a moocher and living off Emily. Not true. He had more money than Emily. He no longer had to work.

It was implied that he paid his half-brother and a friend to help cover this up. This was not true. He was accused of being an alcoholic. Not true. He was accused of being physically violent. Not true. They took something that happened in his twenties and blew it up.

The prosecuting team had numerous people in the court room. Matt's side of the courtroom was sparse, but I later learned that a young friend and his parents were turned away by a deputy before getting in for the trial. Why is unclear. Most of Matt's friends lived in Las Vegas. Sadly, by trial time, Matt's dad had died. Toward the end of the trial, he had family fly in that was in the courtroom.

I am a repurpose sort of gal and have never liked to waste money. Frugal. As a retired employee of a government/county job, I used to be concerned with all the tax dollars that were wasted. I saw people promoted to positions where I felt favoritism played a key role. This trial was a disgrace. A prime example of wasted tax dollars.

So, each day, twenty-one witnesses took the stand for the State and swore to tell the truth, I continued to wait for something to convince me he had possibly killed her. Professional doctors, Pathologists, Anthropologist, Professors, certified people of various expertise had taken the stand. Cops, detectives and several more police officers took the stand.

Many individuals admitted under oath to being paid vast amounts of money to testify. This trial should not have happened. The tax money and time of this trial was amazing. The defense team had only two people take the stand. It wasn't necessary because the prosecuting team had no evidence.

When I started thinking about writing this book, I thought about keeping his verdict until the end. But, because this case became a high- profile case, people watched it from all over the world, and on Dateline.

I have an abundance of friends who tease me about *telling it like it is.* I am outspoken and when I see things that are wrong, I look for change to make it right. I see things either black or white and I won't see any color without clarity. The clarity was "no evidence."

As you read it, you will see it is written from my views alone. I wrote the trial as best I could from my experience from day one, until the end. Some facts/dates could be off slightly, or a quote off by a word or two, but nothing changes the context. This book is about the facts of this horrible ordeal that Matt went through.

My opinion is also included on things about the trial, simply because they are my views and how I felt.

You will see where I address him mostly as Matt because he has become a friend to my husband and I. Emily is also sometimes called by her last name, Noble, but mostly Emily. I feel close to her in an odd way. I think I would have liked her.

I refer to the prosecution also as the state. I don't always identify which of the three for the prosecutor is talking and refer to them as "The Prosecuting team." I, by no means, set out specially to offend anyone. I am aware all the attorneys are highly educated and smart.

I have used fictitious names for the witnesses and attorneys battling against and for Matt. However, this trial can be found all over the internet and each day of the trial can be viewed also.

Matt said to me, "Some people will always feel I did it, I can't change that." He is right, but much of my motivation in writing this was hopefully to share additional information that the public never heard and explain some situations better. Maybe I will change some views. He didn't care how I wrote it, or what I included. He had nothing to hide. "Just write the truth and what you think," he said.

I didn't need his opinion or permission. I just felt like he needed to know and deserved respect, which he hasn't gotten for a long time. Other than learning about him prior to being arrested, I asked for help about his life growing up and prior to Emily. My book is my words, my thoughts, and my opinion.

We all have opinions and freedom of speech but maybe after reading this book, you will understand and see that Matheau Moore is free for a reason. He did not kill his wife and he loved her. As I said on the news, "I will go to my grave knowing we made the right decision."

I hope you enjoy this book and never have to go through anything like this because being accused of such a horrid crime and possibly serving life in prison when innocent would be the worst. I want to believe there are many great police officers and detectives out there. We are all human and they can make mistakes, too. Matheau Moore deserves his name back.

Will I ever wish to serve as a juror again? I don't know, but we, the jurors got it right, I believe, and I still believe, in the judicial system, although I feel it is run like a business, pockets filled sometimes, when they should not have been. Many pockets were filled but not Matt's. Matt is a free man at a high cost and Emily's spirits at rest. God bless her soul.

CHAPTER 1
MATHEAU MOORE—THE BEGINNING

He wasn't a wife killer, and it took a lot of hell and hope, but Matheau L Moore was a decent human who lived a normal, ordinary childhood and adult life. He has a name and deserves it back.

From New York to Las Vegas, to Westerville, Ohio and back running to Las Vegas, Matheau couldn't wait to leave Ohio.

Westerville is a city in Franklin and Delaware Counties, northeast suburb mostly of Franklin County/Columbus, Ohio.

It is a respected, quaint relatively smaller town compared to the big city life. It is said to be one of the best places to live in Ohio. There are many shops, pubs, specialty shops downtown, and great parks to walk or jog. Westerville, in the old downtown area, is quiet, unique and has that suburban feel. It is home to Otterbein University, a liberal arts college.

The chances of becoming a victim of a violent crime in Westerville, is slim. The crime rate is 2.5 times lower than the US average.

Matheau Moore and Emily Noble lived in an upscale condominium area with many neighbors, a wonderful park, and a circular walkway for exercising, walking dogs, a community pool and just a friendly atmosphere. It was common to see them walking and enjoying foraging for wild edible plants to eat. They enjoyed picnics with neighbors, Emily loved working in her yard and always planting various flowers or weeds to take root for eating. They loved walking downtown, too.

Emily was a Neat-Knick. Their home was spotless, and everything had its place. The garage was cleaner than many homes. Matt respected her wishes, and everything was put back in its place.

But let us get to the beginning. Matt was born January 30th, 1971 in Illion, New York, a small village near Utica, New York. His parents met in college, and both graduated from Mohawk Valley Community College as did Matt. He had one older brother, Brian.

Matt lived a typical childhood-a happy home. They were Irish Catholic. Life was good growing up. He was an outdoor kid who loved sports and had an artistic side. Matt admits to being just an average, academic student but a good kid. His home was drug free, rarely had alcohol in it and absolutely no crime. "Just a happy, upper class, privileged life," he said.

"I had a car that my dad bought me. I didn't have to work but I chose to work a few summer jobs and some jobs after school. Money was always around so working was not a necessity. My dad owned his own business in the computer industry. He developed the advanced land line/push button telephone upgrade which began the push button to different departments." Matt's first job as a kid was washing dishes in a restaurant.

His parents divorced when he was about three and his dad moved to Dallas, Texas, but he was always a big part of Matt's life. He spent summers with his dad and never missed holidays with him. His mom remarried and to this day, Matt has a great relationship with his stepdad who he refers to as his second dad.

How blessed Matt was when his dad also remarried and he had a wonderful stepmom, too. He had an older half-brother, Paul, who was a big part of his court battle. He stood by Matt's side never wavering or doubting Matt's innocence. His dad had two additional children when he remarried, and Matt never felt left out.

He likes to call his family Classic American Liberals. "Not like Classic liberals today," he said. His mom had eleven siblings and they all grew up to be outstanding, educated adults. There were always books around and that continued while raising Matt and his older brother, Brian. They attended a Catholic private school until sixth grade and then on to a public high school.

Matt's first girlfriend was in seventh grade, and he recalls feeling awkward around girls. "I was afraid of them. They made me nervous," he said with a chuckle. But my first true relationship was in high school with what I thought was love. She was Hawaiian and we dated a year until she moved away. "I always had girlfriends, and some broke my heart."

During his junior year he was in a tragic accident. It was common back then. "Kids had parties and we drank. I got in the car with the wrong kid and three people got killed."

Matt was hospitalized for about two months with major surgeries, major fractures, and on a respirator.

"That really changed my life. I never got in a car again with drinkers. I continued to party a little, but it was very uncharacteristic of me to drink after that when I was young."

Sadly, his brother was also hit by a drunk driver and died when Matt was fifteen. Brian was only sixteen and it was so difficult for the family to deal with the loss of him in such a senseless way.

"Our family has been through a lot and my faith must have prepared me for this. Seeing pictures of Emily and the way Westerville Police Department treated me, I am not sure how I contained myself during the trial," Matt said.

With all he has lost over the years, he has become stronger mentally.

Matt says he sees people today getting so upset about trivial things and he likes to tell them to hang in there, but he thinks about what all he has been through. "I'm not pre-determinism but I like to think all this happened for a reason. Maybe this can change things."

Sadly, law enforcement can truly get it wrong and make mistakes. Some possibly are incompetent. I have learned many people go to prison for crimes they did not commit. Some victims do not have the resources or money to obtain a good attorney. When I was chosen to be a juror on this case and as I sat through eight days of a trial, it frustrated me and saddened me that Matt had been put through so much.

As Matt said to me, "Maybe this is why you, and I connected, and I agreed for you to write my book." We all want to believe in law enforcement but this battle for freedom is a prime example of the wrong that was done to Emily Noble and Matteau Moore. So, my story continues.

As soon as he graduated from college with a degree in electronics, he hired on shortly after at one of the first Indian Reservations casinos in New York. He worked a year there. He and his college girlfriend had broken up and he and many of his coworkers had decided to move to Vegas for a job opportunity in the casinos there. He moved there in 1995 where he continued to work as a crap dealer for 20 years. "The money was great."

It was in Vegas when he met his first wife. "She was a dancer in a strip club." His son Palmer, who was named after his brother Brian Palmer, was born and sadly died of a bronchi spasm, related to SIDS. He was two years old. Their relationship struggled during the ten years they were together.

His wife never danced again and became a server in a restaurant. "Palmer's death was a dark time."

They separated, would get back together, and try to make things work. Back and forth the relationship went. Matt was lonely and so sad about the loss of Palmer. He had no family in Vegas and running back to her was the only thing he had to try to do to find comfort. Another child was conceived, they decided to marry and subconsciously Matt thought it might help save their relationship.

"His wife became violent and was always hitting me," Matt said. "She was just a violent person. I was never brought up to hit a woman and never saw that ever as a child. It was just awful how we went back and forth, and I would come back to her, hoping to work things out. There she was pregnant, and I wanted things to work out."

Matt always worked the third shift, and he recalled one afternoon stopping by to see his wife.. They had been separated again and he admitted he had been drinking. An argument broke out, blame thrown about Palmer's death, and she hit him which was not unusual. After many years of this, Matt reacted and wrapped his arms around her throat and said, "Stop, just stop. No more hitting."

She called 911 and Matt just sat down. He waited, knowing and assuming he would be the one to look like the perpetrator and all the abuse he had taken over the years would go to deaf ears. He was very aware in Vegas that if someone called in a domestic, someone would spend time in jail. How often do women go to jail for beating up a man?

Matt watched the police. It was obvious to Matt, they judged him and assumed he was at fault. He knew he would be sent off to jail. "I was handcuffed and arrested. I was in a fight once as a teen, but this was my first time going to jail. I spent two days in jail. I got out, ran right back to her, we made up, and she never ever hit me again."

Matt got a letter in the mail and for whatever reason, the charges were dropped, and he never went to court.

In 2001, Joey was born but it couldn't save the marriage and when Joey was about one year old, they divorced. Rarely do marriages go the distance with such a traumatic loss of a child, they called it quits.

"We were just different people. We were young and it was obvious it was time to move on with our lives. We had tried," Matt said.

Matt was always a "stand up dad, in Joey's life, paying child support and being a part of his young life. "My parents were always in my life and Dad would work in Texas and his home in Rochester, New York and always made sure to be in my life. I knew I just always wanted to be around for Joey."

Joey got the best of everything. "Being a dealer, money was never an issue. I didn't like dealing but the money was too good. Working holidays and weekends wasn't fun. I am a family man and working all those holidays just wasn't easy."

"I did meet many famous people. James Wood sat at my table for hours. Once he came and no one else was at my table and I dealt to him all day and we talked and talked. He was a brilliant guy, and so funny."

"Vinny, a drummer for Pantera was at my table a few times. I'm a metal head and he was a drummer. I knew him immediately when he walked up to my table. We talked music as I dealt."

CHAPTER 2
RIP, JOEY

Matt and his ex-wife had shared parenting and by middle school age, Joey started showing signs of mental illness. They continued living in Vegas and Matt was still dealing at a casino. The money was great, and he was saving a lot of money.

Joey was constantly causing trouble at school. His grades were struggling but the school continued to pass him. Matt began home schooling Joey in an effort to get Joey back on track. That was difficult working the hours Matt worked and Joey went back to public school.

By the end of eighth grade, the public school he attended wanted him to repeat eighth grade. Joey was upset. "No way am I going back to eighth grade and leave my friends," he said.

At that time, Matt's dad had retired and was living in Worthington, Ohio and was doing well financially. Matt's dad had divorced his second wife years prior, living alone and wanted to help Matt and Joey. Matt's dad recommended they move to Ohio, get Joey enrolled in public school in Worthington and just see if the change would help.

Joey and Matt thought it was a great idea. So, Matt quit his job and off to Ohio they went in October 2015." Joey took special classes to go at his own pace and things were looking better. Joey was happy and he had an extended family along with his grandpa to spend time with. He was making friends. Matt took a job at the recently opened casino in Columbus, Ohio.

Matt was on a dating app in Vegas. Dating there is different and difficult. People work crazy hours, 24 hours a day, Vegas was alive with so much action. People moved there, left, came back and it was a different lifestyle. When he moved to Ohio, he continued his interest in finding a special woman or to at least have a companion.

Plenty of Fish was the dating app and that was the beginning of his life with Emily Noble in late 2015.

"We met in this dive bar. It was kind of funny, that bar, but we fell in love fast. She was kooky like me, and we just hit it off," Matt said. "I worked and we dated while Joey and I lived with my dad."

Matt had full custody by then. Joey continued to be up and down mentally. Matt was able to recognize his moods. "He was an excellent guitar player and when he was down, he didn't play." Matt knew something was wrong and nothing was getting done to help him just to be stable.

As Matt and Emily's relationship grew, he met some of her family and introduced Joey to her family. The three of them would occasionally go to dinner and they had met extended family also. Matt never had the opportunity to meet Emily's dad. He had passed away from a fall on a ladder about a year before Matt came to Ohio, but he got to know her mom. "We hit it off, she was a sweet lady," he said.

Emily's sister was happy about her sister's new relationship. The families seemed to be blending.

But sadness followed Emily. She was depressed a lot. With all Emily had been dealing with and having a new relationship with Matt, she continued to be smothered with demons. Matt was a people pleaser and he tried constantly to help her and knew her triggers.

Her mom died suddenly in an automobile accident, June 2016. It was terribly hard on Emily. The sudden loss of her mom was difficult and so tragic. Emily, Joey, and Matt attended the funeral as a couple/family.

"Her mom slammed her car into the back of a big truck in the middle of the day. She was not dealing well with the loss of her husband, but the wreck was determined to be just an accident, Matt said. "I am not implying anything, but it was strange."

Emily was close to her mom and dad; she was the only one present with her dad when he took his last breath. She spoke a lot about that, and it was a very spiritual thing for her to talk about death. "One of the first places she took me was to the hospice facility where her dad had passed away. We walked a peaceful path there. It was odd that she took me there, but Emily was different and had such a spiritual side."

Emily began to confide in Matt and told him about sexual abuse she had experienced as a child from someone close. This went on for years when she was a small child and she had kept this awful secret to herself for years.

With both parents gone, Emily had this strong desire to release all the pitted-up secrets. She spoke at length to her sister. It was like the Pandora box opening and all the tainted air coming out.

Seemed like clouds hung over Emily. She was married once and had been alone, widowed since 2011. Her first husband had committed suicide. Emily never talked about it much but told Matt that they never had marital trouble and it was a total shock when he did it.

"Emily told me, he was just a sad guy," Matt said, "She was never attracted to normal people. Emily was a sad person, too. Heck, I am different, maybe that is why we connected. We were both good people...simply different, but we also met at a complicated time. We both had losses. Emily was struggling with guilt over her husband's suicide."

Matt noticed that her depression ran deep, and she truly needed expert help, and he knew he was not able to bring her out of that dark tunnel. He had so many issues to deal with trying to help Joey. Emily was lost and truly didn't seem to want to continue the relationship or get help. Emily was troubled horribly about the sexual abuse. Her constant sadness and demands were weighing him down.

"I never really wanted to leave but she was so consumed and angry at the world, I felt she didn't want us around. I had hoped my leaving might help her to seek help."

With Emily's agreement, Matt decided to move Joey back to Vegas. Emily and Matt had tried. His dad was incredibly supportive of the idea if he thought it would help Joey to go home…back to Vegas. As the months went by, nothing seemed to improve.

Life was so up and down. Matt was trying to work, Joey was a teen, and able to be home alone at night, but Matt worried about him. Should he be home alone? He had never mentioned suicide, but the thoughts lingered for Matt.

Matt and Emily continued a long-distance connection through Facebook.

Joey's mom, was not much help and Matt felt so alone as a parent. There were times when Matt thought Joey was getting better but looking back now, Matt thinks he was good at disguising it.

With that and dealing with constant issues with Joey, Matt was on the brink of helplessness. One sweltering summer day in 2017, Matt was feeling lost, defeated, and befuddled, when his phone rang. He was at one of the lowest times in his life trying to figure out what to do. He looked down and it was Emily. His heart sang. Matt was so excited to talk to her and eager to catch up.

It was as if she had this sixth sense that he needed her. Matt proceeded to give her an update on Joey, and she said with no hesitation…. "Come back, come back, and let me help.

We can get married; I have good insurance, and we can help Joey."

He cried and cried and was so happy she wanted them to come back. Matt thought this was the answer to his prayers.

They loaded the car up and off to Ohio they went…again with hope and happiness. With Emily's inheritance from her mom's death, she bought her siblings out and moved into her mom's condominium.

"She did seem better," Matt said. They married August 18, 2018, and began to enjoy life but constantly observing, supporting Joey. Emily was right there to help. Joey had his own room, and the condominium was on a quiet street.

Emily being such a neat, orderly person had some adapting to do to get used to having two men now living with her. Matt has one word that described Emily and he said she was "Particular." Everything had to be her way, and everything had its place. She was not interested in living with anyone unless they could fit into her demands and be just what she wanted. Matt became that guy and tried for blissfulness with Emily.

"She wasn't mean like my first wife; I loved her, but it was difficult to get along with her, but I tried and loved to see Emily happy."

Matt remembers coaching Joey about putting the toilet lid down, picking up after himself. It was a compromising time for all. He knew if Joey and Emily were happy, it could be smooth sailing.

Emily was big-hearted and jumped in with both feet to welcome Joey back and help him. That fall of 2018, Matt's mom lost her battle with cancer. He inherited a large amount of money. He could live wonderfully comfortable for the rest of his life. Retirement began after 25 years working at casinos. Rebuilding his relationship with Emily, nurturing and guiding Joey full time and taking care of their home became his role. Emily chose to continue to work although they were both set for life financially. So, they thought.

Matt had dated many women, but he had never met a woman like Emily. The women he dated over the years were always full of drama and Matt was constantly giving in or leaving, dating another with issues. Matt's mom called him a people pleaser, so he touched many thorns before the rose.

Matt enjoyed intelligent conversation, music, old movies and loved to have constructive debates. Matt, being a liberal, had many views on our government. Emily worked for the government but didn't trust the government and all their policies. She was very political and even took Matt to a political rally. They could engage politically, and she loved history and there was so much substance to her, and Matt loved that about her.

Matt loved the outdoors and was somewhat of an *old hippy*. They enjoyed listening to podcasts about nature, reading and Matt played guitar, as they grew closer.

She loved it when rain was falling from the skies. Metal buckets would line the driveway to collect it. Matt helped. They would simmer collected foraged weeds with the rainwater. They called it Rainwater Soup which Matt learned was delicious.

Emily was his perfect match. They shared many talks and walks. There was a beautiful walkway, and parks were abundant. Emily helped him appreciate silent walks in the woods which they did daily and reminded him how being in nature was uplifting. From birds to feeling the wind, it helped Emily. Her soul had been so scarred from much sadness and she wanted to heal, be happy. Her mood swings were often, but Matt pushed on. It was nothing and easier than dealing with the physical abuse of his first wife.

Emily loved sex and she expected Matt to make love to her every night. Matt had dated another girl years ago who had been sexually abused and he felt these sexual expectations were intertwined with their past. He noticed if he weren't interested, she would become angry.

Emily loved to garden and enjoyed her yard, always pulling and inspecting weeds. She foraged and loved repurposing weeds into healthy foods and soups. They collected rainwater for drinking and took vitamins. They had no plastic in their home and lived a very organic life.

Joey was a constant worry. He felt his life was worthless and he heard voices in his head. There were also times Matt thought Joey was getting better. Looking back, Matt thought Joey was probably just good at putting on a front to not cause worries for his dad and Emily.

Doctors, counseling, guidance counselors, teachers were all involved with Joey again and they continued to look for answers. And then, Joey was diagnosed with Schizophrenia. He was in and out of hospitals, different medications tried and there they were, parents of a teen with severe mental illness. "It was such a difficult time," Matt said.

The word was spoken aloud one evening and Matt's heart sunk. Joey mentioned the word, suicide and we were like, "NO. No, Joey."

Mental illness is confusing. Doctors treat it with medicine, but no one truly knows where it comes from. "He wasn't the son I remembered anymore, it was so sad as the changes came and I felt like I hardly knew him anymore."

Matt and Emily worried constantly. Joey would leave and they had the worries of wondering if he would come back through the door. "After some discussion, we had ourselves convinced if he would ever do something like this, it would certainly not be in his teens, maybe later in life. But the worries were constant."

Emily left on a trip with a friend. This trip had been planned long before Matt and Joey came back. Joey was working a part time job and Matt scheduled a golf outing with his dad.

It was the day that Matt's life changed forever. He had tried calling Joey to check on him and decided to play golf anyway. After all, Joey was seventeen and it was not out of the realm for one his age to be gone for hours. Worries sometimes can be just that and Joey would walk through the door later.

They had just started playing when he received a call from the Westerville Police Department, and they asked him to come down to the station. They handed Matt Joey's cell phone, and he looked up at them and said, "Where is Joey?"

Turned out a jogger had found Joey hanging. "Dad took me to get a twelve pack of beer, took me home and there I sat. I knew I had to let Emily know. I texted her and she headed home."

Matt was ridiculed and later in court the prosecuting team tried to make him look uncaring and cold in how he managed giving the sad news to Emily.

Emily came back and that night, Emily accepted Matt's sadness as he rolled over to try to sleep with no desire for sex. "It was the first time it was not demanded of me."

They had a beautiful spiritual celebration of Joey's life at a skate park. Kids came from everywhere, many who didn't know Joey but came to honor his life.

Emily and I did amazingly well together as we tried to heal and lean on each other. "She did everything for me and allowed me to mourn my way with no pressure." As time went on, Matt continued to not have a desire for sex. "I do think our sexless marriage was part of the reason she committed suicide."

As an adult, Matt drank but he considered himself a happy drinker, and rarely a *sloppy drunk*. He drank more, his moods were up and down, missing Joey so much. His interest in sex died. Many times, during the night, he would wake up, needing to go to the bathroom and would go to Joey's bed. He had learned over the months that Emily's sleep was important, and she did not like to be awakened.

By then the Covid epidemic happened and Emily began to work from home. Matt was happy to have her home with him as they were trying to adjust to their loss. Matt continued to not have a desire for sex which bothered Emily a lot. He loved her so much, but his sadness ran deep for Joey. Losing a child is the ultimate loss and he had lost two.

Matt began to blame, he blamed himself, he blamed Emily, he was struggling for answers when they had tried so hard to help Joey. One night, Matt lashed out at Emily, and she stomped out, into the garage. Matt sat and sobbed on the couch. Minutes went by and he went to the garage to check on her.

Hanging from an extension cord was Emily. She had tied it off and was hanging unconscious. Matt immediately lifted her down, cut the rope off and carried her into the house. She gasped, breathed and he carried her to bed where he lay beside her as they wept.

"The next morning, I asked her if she wanted to talk about what she had done. I told her I was sorry, and Joey's death was not our fault."

She said, "I just wanted to see if I could do it."

Matt only told one person the next day about this. He called one of his best friends, Mark from Georgia. Matt was torn about not calling the Westerville police officers that night before, but he was not happy with the way they had treated him with Joey's death. He decided he would watch Emily closely; not leave her alone.

It would be later after his arrest that he did tell his defense team about the attempt Emily had made in the garage, but it would never be used because it would be considered hearsay.

"Things started getting better, "he said.

So, he thought.

CHAPTER 3
THE LAST DANCE

May 24th, 2020 was to be one of the best days of Matt's life. They had begun filtering their water and getting healthy was the top priority for them. Matt had recently spoken to his stepdad who suggested they take a drive to Buchtel, Ohio to check out the spring water there. Emily told Matt she would like to go there for her birthday.

They took many glass bottles to collect water to take home. It was a beautiful day full of promise. They stopped at a rest stop; ate lunches they had packed. The sun was shining, and it was a perfect day.

On their way back home, they decided to stop and visit Matt's dad. His dad had allowed them to plant a big garden on his property. Emily was excited to work in her garden and couldn't wait for the vegetables to grow. Matt helped his dad with a line that had busted in his yard. He fixed the broken line. His dad had a friend over, they sat in the yard and listened to him play his guitar.

The day was still early. They decided to go home to clean up, change clothes and head to the field of flags and take some pictures, thinking about the veterans. Emily decided she wanted to go out to some bars and continue the celebration of her birthday. They headed to uptown Westerville.

The Covid mask requirement had lifted, and people were going out again.

The next stop was one of the local bars they liked to go to occasionally. The bar was not as busy like the old days, pre-Covid. But some were out. They met a group of young guys, maybe in their twenty's and recalled one older man with them. He remembered being surprised at how friendly they were when they approached Matt and Emily. They shared laughs and stories and were having a wonderful time….so much that they decided to head on to Jimmy V's Grill and Pub, another familiar bar they had been to before.

Matt was not accustomed to meeting friendly people in Westerville. Living in Vegas for so many years, he was used to a friendly, social atmosphere. It was normal in Vegas for strangers to buy drinks for all. He felt Westerville people were just stand off-ish, different.

This group they met was not your typical hoity-toity from Westerville. They were heavy drinkers, dressed very casually and just did not seem to be locals. But they did not send bad vibes to Matt and Emily. It was just a fun experience welcomed by Matt who missed that welcoming atmosphere.

At trial when they were going over the timeline talking about the places Matt and Emily had been to, I wondered if the police officers questioned these people that Matt and Emily had hung out with. They did not testify.

Although it appeared they were just a party group of out of towners who were harmless, how did Westerville PD know this without questioning them? Wouldn't they be people of interest since they were some of the last to see Matt and Emily?

The last place they stopped to eat was at a popular restaurant in downtown Westerville, called The Old Bag of Nails. That server was called to testify. Why? The prosecuting team had her on the stand for about 45 minutes and she served no purpose. She saw nothing, she had nothing of importance to say.

Prop Witness? A filler? As a juror I had not heard these terms, but it was obvious we would begin hearing testimony from many who truly had no evidence on Matt. It seemed the prosecuting team were trying to find anything that might *stick*.

Prop witnesses take up time and spend money. The more witnesses, the more time, the more days, the more money spent and some getting richer. Tax dollars, Matt's money, was it political moves to impress their town? They needed someone to go down. Residents were very concerned.

Matt ate and suggested they take a serious selfie. That picture became a negative tool for the prosecuting team who tried to analyze and imply that Matt and Emily were fighting. It was simply a picture taken in fun because Matt was enjoying trying to get Emily to not smile and look mean in the picture.

Maybe the server/bartender saw them posing, laughing, making silly faces, looking menace as they snapped pictures. What kind of evidence was that and why was she subpoenaed to court? For what? She served no purpose.

There never was a fight. "Emily and I didn't fight, ever. There were many times she would try to pick a fight, and she could not get a fight out of me. That is just not me."

Emily had the swing moods and was difficult at times, but Matt was easy going and he spent more time trying to keep peace and would constantly compromise.

"She was worth it, and that day was one of the best days of my life. I didn't think about Joey, and I felt free of grief, and we just had so much fun."

It was about 6:45 PM and the sun was going down. The neighbor that lived across from Matt and Emily saw them come home that night.

They talked in the kitchen. Matt called a friend. He browsed through his phone, made small talk with Emily and off to bed. A nightly ritual was going to bed together and Matt ending up in Joey's room later. He didn't dare want to wake

Emily. He respected her wishes about sleep and after getting up to go to the bathroom, Matt would end up in Joey's room that night, also.

He recalled getting up again during the night to go to the bathroom, he had assumed Emily was in bed in the master bedroom. He went back to Joey's room.

That morning, a Tuesday, Emily was gone. Just gone. In the evening after speaking to Emily's good friend and neighbor, it was decided to call Westerville PD who came and took a report.

This was a big thing in the relatively small town of Westerville. Crime rates were low, and murders were less. Big news, big stuff, and enthusiastic police officers with something big time, out of the norm to do.

A celebration for Emily's 52nd birthday had ended with much happiness and who would have thought it would be the last with such a sad ending?

Matheau Moore would become the small fish in a big pond of sharks.

CHAPTER 4
THEY MADE HIM JAILBAIT

After Matt had talked to police officers and they had written the report, Matt genuinely thought Emily would come home. Maybe there was some lack of communication, or something. It just didn't make sense.

So worried about Emily, he decided to reach out to a well-known reality show that helped find missing people. Matt was sure she was alive. He paid them $10,000.00. They said they would broadcast it to various news stations to help get people all over the nation to look for her.

Everything on the news implied she was dead and made Matt look more guilty. He started thinking everything and everybody was all about making money. They did nothing but cash his check and it made it look worst in the public eye for Matt.

A friend of Matt's told him about a true crime podcast that's goal is to look for missing people. Matt called them, and they gave him an extensive interview. Sadly, they took his information and twisted it to make Matt look awful. It served no purpose but to help feed the public with negative untruths, and speculations about Emily's disappearance and making him look guilty.

It was a Wednesday, just less than two days since she had disappeared, the Westerville PD came to Matt's house with a search warrant, took his phone and he was placed in the back of their cruiser like a criminal. He was cooperative and wanted to go in to help find Emily. He asked several times if they knew something or had found her. They would not give him an answer, so Matt went looking and hoping for answers. But once inside the police station, their attitude towards him changed quickly; he was read his Miranda Rights and he realized it was an interrogation. He felt the nasty looks and knew their motive was not to help Matt find Emily alive, but it was to find Emily dead and accuse him of murder.

They spoke to him for about two hours, accusing him of killing her. He probably said too much but he just wanted to help. Matt had nothing to hide. As he has said many times, "I just told the truth. I guess when you are innocent and don't have the mind of a criminal, you are just yourself." Matt said.

They were in his face and trying to break him down. When he was released, he couldn't believe it. Within less than 48 hours, Westerville PD decided Emily was dead and he had done it.

"They blew it. I would have been so cooperative in helping find Emily, but they had already alienated me and already decided I was guilty of a crime," Matt said.

Since Emily's disappearance, harsh judgement and insinuations were daily from the neighborhood. Emily just disappeared and just like that they all assumed Matt had killed her. Matt rarely left the condominium.

Matt's half-brother, Paul came to Westerville immediately from Florida to be with Matt and a good friend, Art. They were concerned and aware from updates from Matt that the police officers were after him. They spent 11 days with Matt in support of him and were concerned for Emily's disappearance.

"I don't know what I would have done if they hadn't come to be with me," Matt said. "That was the nicest thing anyone could have done for me."

Matt didn't have many friends in Westerville. He had spent most of his life in other states. The few friends he had met through Emily had turned on him.

Matt was talking to his family and friends, and they were all so worried for Matt and how the Westerville PD were suspecting him. His family and friends all kept telling him he would be okay and giving him support, trying to keep him positive.

Matt made up fliers and the three of them set out passing them out and posting them all over. They never felt like they were looking for a body. They were simply trying to find Emily. Matt stayed home on some days as people came to pick up fliers. He also thought Emily would walk in unexpectedly just like she had walked out with no goodbye, no note, just gone.

Since Westerville PD had kept his phone, he had bought another, talking daily to his dad and numerous friends who lived out of state. Matt heard weird noises in the background on his phone and wondered if his phone was being tapped. He talked freely. He had nothing to hide.

He had gone into the police department thinking he was helping, and they had him signing his Miranda rights document. Matt became paranoid, and he felt like a ticking time bomb. Some evenings he would see lights beam into his house. Instead of out looking for a suspect or for Emily possibly alive, they were immediately pointing towards him, and he knew he was being watched.

Later in court, we jurors learned that a GPS was placed on his car without his knowledge. They finally removed it when they found nothing. And if his phone were tapped, they would have found nothing, or I would have assumed that would have been used against him in court. He talked on his phone for a year before he was arrested.

Matt had not hired an attorney yet but got some free advice from a friend of a friend's civil attorney. "Don't go on the searches with all the groups that are searching daily and do not talk to the cops," the lawyer told him. "Go on your own searches."

He took the advice of that attorney and would not talk to the police officers again to give them any opportunity to twist his words.

He missed Emily so much and just couldn't understand where she was and why. They had so much fun on her birthday and Matt didn't see any sign of unhappiness on that last evening he spent with her.

Sleep was difficult. He was lonely but truly had no fear. He knew he was innocent and was just sure everything would be figured out. By then Paul and Art had to get back home. They just couldn't stay any longer.

That made the condominium quieter. He became so sad and upset that Emily would leave. It even crossed his mind that she had ran off with some guy. But that just didn't seem possible.

There was never a trust issue. They had so much sadness and trauma in both their lives, but they were helping to hold each other up. He just couldn't believe she was gone.

Just weeks after her disappearance, Matt hired a private investigator who talked to the neighbor across the street. That neighbor told the investigator he had seen Emily on Monday morning, the day she disappeared. But that information served no purpose in the trial because his story changed. In fact, it was told in court that the neighbor had immediately told the police officers he did not see her on Monday. He had; he saw her on Monday but why did his story change?

CHAPTER 5
THE OVERZEALOUS SWAT TEAM

If you talk about the biggest action ever in Westerville, June 18, 2021, was the day. As Matt was pulling out of the condominium complex, broad day light, the police officers approached his car heavily armed. They looked like a swat team about to make a bust of a huge cartel organization. They surrounded his car all armed with some kind of semi-automatic guns, hollering for him to get out of his car with his hands up. It was 13 months for the arrest to be made.

The media blew it up as I looked back on it after the trial and listened to replays of it from the news, it was odd I had never heard anything about it prior to being selected as a juror. We were too busy enjoying our great life, loving all the new grandbabies as each was born, watching them, and loving retirement. We were just busy living our slower paced life since retiring and just being "us."

They all had on, protective gear from head to toe, including bullet proof chest protectors. Wow, this was big stuff in a low crime town. Matt was very cooperative as he had been since this all began.

I remember the newspaper annually putting a special edition out at the end of each year about the biggest things that happened for the year in our county. This story was not mentioned. Why? My guess is they wanted it to go away.

"All they had to do was ask me to come in," Matt said. He had been under surveillance for just over a year. He saw this coming.

Money certainly couldn't be the motive; Matt had inherited over $600,000.00. Motive couldn't be an affair going on. They had watched him and had a GPS on his car. Neighbors were spying, also to keep the police officers informed prior to the arrest. Matt wasn't sneaking women in and wasn't doing anything wrong.

Westerville PD spent a lot of time and money looking for an expert who would find Emily's death to be a strangulation, and boom. Matt became their guy. The locals were probably relieved, and the town gossip might settle down. Matt was the easiest and obvious target.

Once in jail, Matt's dad took money out of Matt's inheritance to retain an attorney because the Westerville PD had frozen Matt and Emily's joint checking account which had over $100,000.00 in it. I personally still wonder how they can freeze accounts if someone has not been convicted. I was learning things about the law; I also was learning how things just seemed wrong even if it was legal. Matt would need big bucks to fight for freedom. Thank goodness for his dad who could help.

Matt was frightened and felt defeated. On the second day in jail, he was charged, and the bond set was 2.5 million dollars. That sure did not help his mood. He fought for sanity and to dig deep for hope.

The first two weeks he was placed in solitary confinement. Matt assumed this was a suicide watch. The room was about eight feet by eight feet. All alone, all day, all night. They let him out for about 30 minutes each day to walk some and to shower.

Being confined and with no one to talk to, and under so much pressure, Matt felt like he was losing his mind. When he was allowed out each day for a small amount of time, he would call his dad. He had trouble focusing on conversations. The pressure and being in jail were maddening.

The security guards gave him books which he was glad to have. He loved to read and although the books were not great, he was glad to have something to read.

When he was sent out of solitary, he was placed in the violent criminal section. "A pod," is what he called it. The first thing he did was look for someplace to hang a sheet to kill himself. He was so frightened, and he knew if things got bad or he was tortured, he would end his life. He had no idea what to expect.

He kept to himself and stayed quiet. After about a week there, the inmates figured out what he was in for. He took the advice of his attorney who told him to not talk about his case, but the inmates drilled him.

Some even accused him of being a child molester before they heard the actual reason he was in jail. They watched a lot of television and found out from the news what Matt was in for, and they treated him okay. And just like the high-profile case it had become, they felt they were in jail with an interesting guy.

Matt picked up quickly that some inmates wanted to get information from him, because they were *informants.* But he watched what he said. He began talking to some, and they played cards, chess and he read the Bible. Matt loved art and drew a lot. It took some time, but he felt his mind was clearer. He was known as a model prisoner.

And although the food was horrible just as we all hear about jail food; he somehow was surviving. Social media and others wanted to portray Matt as an alcoholic. The only thing he wanted was a good steak someday if that day would ever come.

He was the sole beneficiary of Emily's condominium. With the help of his dad, he was trying to protect what was rightfully his and hired an additional civil attorney who was expensive.

A TOD, transfer on death was on the condo/deed, prior to when Emily married Matt and Emily had put Matt in her will. Matt was to get everything of Emily's and got nothing because Emily had not removed the TOD which still had her sister's name on the deed.

Everyone thought Matt was guilty and he was sure this civil attorney had heard all the talk. Seems they all rub elbows, anyway. Soon he learned that $45,000.00 went down the drain without a resolution for Matt. More money gone with not any or much help and the condominium was gone, too.

From what I learned, he sure as hell did not want to live in that condominium with all that had happened even if he would get out of jail. Westerville would never be his home again and the condo taken away. But it would have been nice to know he would have a nest egg to begin his life again if that could happen.

Matt sat in jail and pondered and did not trust anyone. It was obvious many knew how much money he had, and it seemed he was being misrepresented just like the money he spent on help from the television show. Matt was becoming a smoke screen as his money also was going up in smoke.

Matt had so much doubt in attorneys, but realized he needed to take the advice of the civil attorney and hire a criminal attorney. He needed great representation and to feel positive and find faith.

His new criminal attorney came to jail to talk to Matt on several occasions. That attorney decided to bring in another attorney. Matt became so frustrated and was constantly talking to his dad to keep him updated.

Matt's dad dropped a large amount of money to the second attorney and that was the beginning of Matt's new kick-some- ass -attorney who would be the one to win his case. His first attorney never came back and wasn't in the court room at all for the trial. Rumor was it was due to Covid. Matt was advised to quit working with the private investigator.

Valentina didn't come to see him much at all and he had so much information he wanted her to know. He never felt reassured, and he felt horrified needing to know something or given some reassurance. He had become so paranoid and untrusting of everyone and was sure his money and life would be gone. He'd rot in prison.

He made many calls to his dad and felt the need to talk more to Valentina. Matt asked his dad to call Valentina and to advise her he wished desperately to speak to her. She finally came to the jail and spoke to him. Valentina made it very clear to him she wanted to win.

If things couldn't get any worse, he was called out of his pod to take a call. It was his stepmom. He was shocked and so saddened to learn his dad had died. "I know my dad died of a broken heart," Matt said.

His stepmom then became his lifeline for any help he needed. His dad would never know his son would become a free man. Matt was not able to go to the funeral. Another blow. One blow after another.

Matt met a career criminal in prison who also was working with the same two attorneys. That prisoner gave Matt more faith in thinking he would be found not guilty and to have faith in Valentina. He waited and waited for a trial date.

He had spent 15 months in jail before the trial began. Matt had himself convinced everyone was just taking all his money, no one was doing anything, and he would spend the rest of his life in prison and be known as a wife killer. He had heard tales about women killers and just like child killers, they were judged harshly in prison, and he planned to die. He also thought no one believed him when he stayed true and honest, about being innocent.

"The police officers needed no evidence to convict me, the prosecution needed nothing to arrest me, and a jury didn't need any evidence to indict me, why would I think the jury would find me not guilty? I felt the entire world was against me," Matt said.

And as he had all those thoughts, the jury process began.

CHAPTER 6-DAY 1
THE CHOSEN

I received a juror questionnaire in the mail in July 2020. I was excited. I had always wondered why I had never been called or asked to be on jury duty. My husband had been called and served on a few over the years. We were both consistent at voting at the polls, so why had I never been asked? I had heard over the years they went by car registries, and I sure had cars and tags. So, I thought it might be interesting to finally have the opportunity.

While working full time and raising our children, running kids here, there, and everywhere, I didn't care or give it much thought about possible jury duty. I was too busy.

But retired, working part time, kids grown, it seemed like something I would have time to do. When I received my questionnaire, I immediately filled it out and sent it in. And that is where it all began.

For a few months, I had to call in and each time, I was told on a recording I wasn't needed. (For whatever reason.) By the last date I had to call in, I had decided it was ending and I still would not serve as a juror. I was surprised to hear I was to report in on August 15th 2022. I would possibly become a part of a trial.

When I got to the courthouse, I intuitively knew something big was happening because of all the news media vans and cameras in the parking lot.

As I walked in, the process took several hours and there were about eighty potential jurors. Certainly, I would not be chosen. I was chosen and as we walked into the jury box, we still didn't know what kind of case it was. I assumed it might be something like, someone fighting a red-light citation, or a bar fight and someone opposing their arrest. But then again, why were all those cameras outside? I knew nothing about the law or courts. That was a good thing…my nose has always been clean.

As I sat there, I found it remarkably interesting. The judge, Henry Barnaby, was very professional in a dark suit, had a kind smile, and grey hair explained many things to us, and we understood we could be there for days.

We also were advised to not discuss the trial with our co-jurors or at home with anyone. We were advised not to watch the news, too. At deliberation would be our time to discuss the case.

It was later as we went on breaks, or lunch, I realized how difficult it was to not speak about the trial. I wondered about their thoughts, but we all did an excellent job in sticking to the rules.

Sitting closest to the jury box was the prosecuting team. I noticed three of them, two males and a female attorney who was our Prosecuting attorney for Delaware County. The two men were her assistants.

A third representative was part of the prosecuting team and spoke the least as people took the stand. But it was so odd that this attorney, the weakest link did the beginning and part of the ending statements which seemed odd since Lois Swanson was the leader of the team.

The defense team consisted of two brunette women, both dressed professionally and looked very polished and professional in their business suits. The one caught my attention. She was spunky and passionate. Her name was Abigail Valentina, and she was tough. I noticed this immediately.

At the back of the room stood a deputy (bailiff) who would be in that same spot for days as we listened to this trial.

I noticed what I thought was reporters and right across from me, sitting to the side of the judge was the court reporter who wore very cool shoes. She was always very friendly to us during our trips in and out of the courtroom. Some jurors were excused for assorted reasons as others standing would take the place for the excused one.

I was asked a question by the defense attorney about my job in EMS and she made a comment that I had probably seen a lot in those years working on an emergency squad. I certainly had. After what I saw during the trial, I understood how images could be difficult for jurors to see. I was more upset with the loss of the victim. After twelve jurors and four alternates were chosen, the others were excused, we got down to business.

Sitting with the defense team was the defendant, a middle-aged male, clean shaved with short hair and in a nice dress shirt. He appeared unemotional and sat incredibly quiet, not moving much with his head upward, listening.

From my jury seat, I had a great straight on view of him and wondered as they were going over the pre-trial format, what he was accused of.

Sitting just behind the prosecuting team was Detective Loke who you will hear about later. Remember as you read about the trial, he was given "Top Cop' in December 2020. He had only been a detective a few months and had never been an investigator for a crime to this extent.

I sat next to a female juror, a little older than me. We were a very diversified group of jurors. But when I heard why we were there, I realized I would be spending many days with this group of people. This was not going to be a simple trial. This was far more than a shoplifting case, or a red light or bar fight. Delaware County has always been a fine community to live in. Murders were not something common.

Matheau Moore was accused of killing his wife, Emily Noble and staging her death to look like a suicide. She disappeared on May 25th, 2020 and was not found until September 16th, 2020, by good Samaritans who found her skeleton body partially suspended under a tree by a USB cord near where many had searched for months.

Matt had already served over a year in jail, awaiting his trial. He spent a year prior being questioned, over and over, followed by police officers, and dealing with neighbors and nasty comments on social media.

Emily had not had closure, his life was on the line, and he had many days and months to think, relive things and think about those he loved his thoughts in how he got into this conundrum. He wanted and needed closure for the loss of Emily and to get answers. He needed support from those who could believe in him.

I saw him look over at the jury box, scanned us and probably wondered about us. Would we find him guilty, or would we set him free? This jury experience for me became something more. I felt honored and I realized I had the power along with eleven others to decide the outcome for Matheau Moore. It was so important and a job I planned to do well.

I learned what a side bar was. The only side bar I had experienced was swimming up to the bar in Florida while on vacation. There were many and heard many objections, mostly from Valentina who was working hard to prove his innocence. But I am jumping ahead and will walk through the entire trial.

I stared at him, watched his body language as both teams began their opening arguments on day two. He never expressed any emotions in the beginning. Guilty or not guilty, I thought as I sat there, it would be difficult to not want to react to some of the things being said. But he sat there, quietly.

I would catch him looking down as if he were writing his thoughts or maybe he was drawing to ease his mind. Maybe he was closing it all out, certainly not wanting to be sitting in that seat that could change his life for the better or worse. Maybe he was thinking about Emily or being free, sitting at home, a free man. But whatever his thoughts were, he was in for a long ride as I was also beginning my job as a juror. And this case would have a significant impact on me.

CHAPTER 7
THE WOODS

Prior to the actual first day of the trial, we jurors went on two shuttle type vans to the home at Hummingbird Lane where Matt and Emily had lived. A woman named Carol, who was ever so kind, was our escort. She would be with us daily doing various things for us.

We then went to the actual location where Emily's body was discovered. From Delaware Court in Delaware, Ohio to the very south edge of Delaware County, the ride took about 20-25 minutes. Due to the busy time of day, there was excessive traffic.

The vans parked and as we exited the buses, camera crews were already parked awaiting our arrival. I realized that this was going to be a high-profile case. It was a warm day; the sun was shining.

We were led down a bike path and on to a sidewalk, turning toward County Line Road, a remarkably busy, highly traveled road. We were led down a slight hill, into a wooded area of trees, with thicket and weeds. Looking into the wooded area, it appeared dense and shady. Once we were in and began walking, it was easy to see ahead but still cumbersome.

We dredged ahead and I recall thinking about the jurors older than me. I am not a spring chicken, and I have bad knees and a crappy back. I hoped the older jurors would be okay reaching the spot where Emily was found. Some were sweating.

I would never dare ask for help and continued. We reached the area, we studied the tree, and were told where her body was, how it was positioned. We were not told much more than that at this time. I suspected it was because the council was not there and too much information could sway us one way.

We simply walked back out of the woods, and into the vans and headed back to the courthouse where we would be released for the day. None of the camera crew approached us.

The next day, August 16th, 2022, was the beginning of a trial that would draw attention from people all over the world.

CHAPTER 8
HERE COMES THE JUDGE-DAY 1

Judge Barnaby became a familiar face for the days ahead and his calm, but voice of authority was noticed immediately by me. He reminded us of things we could and could not do.

We were provided tablets and a pen if we wished to keep notes. We were told the tablets full of notes would be destroyed after the trial. They were simply tools we could refer to as the trial proceeded on.

I found taking notes helpful and would look over my notes each day before going home. This tablet was mine to use only at the trial and could not go home with me. Carol told us they were locked up each day and would be returned to us the following morning.

We were told after each witness's testimony; we would be permitted to anonymously write down any question we might have, and it would be shared with both teams. They would sidebar, read our questions, agree to the ones they wanted. Judge Barnaby would then turn and read the question to the witness. Each one was answered, some things clarified with an extended answer and then that witness would step down.

We always had questions…good questions. I later learned after the trial that this was unusual to allow jurors to ask questions. It must have been a customary practice for Judge

Barnaby since some of the attorneys said publicly that this was also a new experience for them. I also learned the judge and defense team thought we had asked interesting, intelligent questions.

The opening statements then began. The State, (Prosecution) was first up. I noticed a red-haired younger man came up from behind the defense team which I thought was odd to make the opening statement. Seemed he would be sitting at the table with Swanson and Stevens, the two prosecuting attorneys. Later as I looked on the county web site, I couldn't find him anywhere.

His name was Michael, and he was young. Was he some soon-to-be attorney? Was he an attorney who needed some experience? But why would he make the opening statement and not our prosecutors that our tax dollars pay for? They are elected officials. Wouldn't their opening and closing statements be especially important and the best doing that? His representation became a mystery to me.

"I'll be honest with you...." That was how he began. He also said something like, "I like to read the end of a book first." Odd, just odd to me.

He told us that we would hear much testimony from family, friends, and a neighbor. We were encouraged to pay attention to the timeline from the evening of May 24, when they went home from their night out, and how he waited until 5:47 PM, the following evening to call Westerville PD. He told us we would learn about how Emily had left without her purse, her cell, her car and had just disappeared. She had left after making the bed that morning.

We would hear about the search for her, that lasted for an entire four months. Numerous people searched, many who didn't even know her. Fliers were made and distributed all around Westerville.

Cell phone forensic would be presented and we would see the discrepancy of the timeline from the time they got home, and she disappeared. I wasn't convinced. The hours

Matt couldn't account for were in the wee hours of the night. His phone was idle. I thought that was a possibility and likely was my thought. But I would wait to hear about this time frame and the crucial hours unaccounted for.

We would hear testimony from the three women who found Emily on September 16th, 2020, who then called Westerville PD. We were warned we would see pictures that were taken on the scene of how Emily's remains were found close to her home, in a kneeling position under a tree that was about 6 ½ feet tall with a USB cord around her neck. He reminded us that numerous searches were done in areas remarkably close to where the three women found her.

We would hear about the physical damage to Emily's body and about the bilateral fractures on her neck and other areas. We would hear about trauma to the nasal bone, top of her lip area. These injuries would be argued by both teams and studied by many experts. Can you imagine being accused of being a wife beater? "I wasn't raised that way," Matt told me later when this book began.

We would hear all this from experts for days. The prosecuting team paid an expert but when they didn't get the results they wanted, they hired another. That expert with the report they didn't like ended up testifying for the defense which helped this case in confirming the suicide.

The prosecuting team spent $1000.00's to find someone to make their case stronger and it still wasn't convincing to us.

Dr. McDaniel was their guy, so they thought. He would testify and explain the cause of death was that of a manual strangulation. He would testify that this was a "staged suicide." He was not a certified medical examiner and later I would get a bad taste in my mouth of his testimony. I would also wonder how much this man was paid. I saw him as someone out to ring his own bell. He had his own personal agenda.

We would also hear about Matt's excuses for the hours between 1-4 AM of May 25th. We would hear that Matt used a "find my app" and started calling friends about noon the day of May 25th, waiting too long in the minds of the prosecuting team. He waited because he was certain nothing horrid had happened. Little did he know, Westerville PD was already suspecting him.

We would hear and see the bodycam from Officer Williams, the first officer who came to talk to Matt, and write up the first official report.

We would see how Matt was accused of staging the scene when they came in with a search warrant unknown to him and as they sifted through his home, Matt noticed something out of place. Emily had trained him and Joey to put things back where they belonged. We heard in court how they turned that and said he was setting the scene for himself.

Most importantly, we would find Matt guilty of killing Emily Noble. Well, that didn't happen, did it?

Next Abigail Valentina, the defense attorney, presented her opening statement. She told us we would see that there is no evidence to convict Matt, and we would see their theory doesn't make sense.

The state would fail to show any physical evidence. We would hear about the huge investigation that was done, the BCI was brought in, and they extensively searched Noble's car, the house, the attic, the bedding, the sheets in Joey's bedroom, more bedding from the master bedroom, the bathroom, the hamper which showed the clothing in the dirty hamper was the same clothing that Matt and Emily wore on the night before when they were out for her birthday. The jean skirt Emily had worn was hanging in her closet after their night out.

She informed us there was no blood, no fiber, no tissue, no DNA, no nothing.

Bodycam would also show the police officers accusing him of murder very soon after coming into his home.

Cadaver dogs, trained specifically for finding bodies, and trained to be alerted of any suspicious smell, were used and nothing was found by the specialized dogs.

Evidence will show Matt had no injuries to his body. He volunteered to go to the police station, as he willingly showed his arms, legs, neck, back, stomach and chest in an effort to prove his innocence and convince them there was not a fight, struggle, scratches, marks of any kind on his person. No blood was found, no bruises, nothing.

As she spoke, she showed images of a wide variety of places inside their home that were studied and swabbed for evidence. Nothing was found in the house, in the attic, in the garage, or in Emily's car. No blood or anything that appeared suspicious.

She told us we would see images of the two of them wearing the clothes they had worn after coming back from the water springs, washing up, changing into for their night out. The selfies captured would validate this.

A GPS was placed unknow to Matt on his car for two weeks and it pulled up nothing of value. They spoke to neighbors, one being a mother that lived near their home and told the officers her kids were outside a lot on May 25th, and they were home all day. She saw or heard nothing. Not one neighbor saw or heard anything.

They spoke to another neighbor who said he saw Emily the morning of May 25th outside. Valentina paced as she continued with her opening. I could tell she was fired up. She looked directly at us in the jury box. and continued about how Emily's remains were found with casual jogging type clothes on, tennis shoes, dressed appropriately for a walk.

Matt told the Westerville Detective where to search. He walked Loke, the head- detective near where Emily's body was found and suggested they go into the wooded area. Loke chose to not go into the wooded area, nor did the other police officers who came to Matt's house.

Instead, they tried to use this against him saying he killed her, or he would have walked down in the wooded area. The public made awful comments on social media. Who would want to walk into the woods, looking for a spouse months after a son had hung himself in a wooded area?

Valentina had the map up on a projector showing the condominium complex along with the woods, bike path, roads, and streets around it. We would end up seeing that map countless times.

She asked us to think about our trip to the scene the day prior and if we noticed the busy area and how much traffic was on County Line Road. Terribly busy at all hours. She reminded us that we should have noticed there was nowhere on this busy road, near the woods to park a car.

The police officers searched the area three times, and with professional dogs, and the BCI was called in to help.

She went on to tell us other things that I took notes on, and I knew I would listen intently to all these testimonies and keep an open mind.

I watched Matt sitting there and saw extraordinarily little emotion. He would write on a pad, write a note, and hand it to Valentina's assistant. I watched him take a mouth lozenge out of a box and put it in his mouth. I observed him purposely to see if I could notice any body language. Looking back, I wonder how he kept his composure so well with all he had to see and hear. The images of Emily were not for the weak to see.

Valentina spoke about Emily who had experienced so much tragedy in her life. She told us Noble had sought counseling and was broken hearted, traumatized over the death of Joey. She felt sad, guilty, and struggled with normal activities, too. She had even taken time off work after Joey's death. She worried about Matt because of his loss of Joey. It was a struggle for him to get out of bed and doing anything was difficult, even the simple things. Noble had a history of anger and depression, and this amplified it.

It was at this moment, I looked at Matt and he teared up and was wiping his nose. I would be lying if I said I didn't feel sorry for him sitting there. I did and I also would feel terribly sorry for Emily when I would later see the images of her and all she had endured through her turbulent life. I felt sadness seeing the images of her tiny little body remains with that cord around her lying alone under the tree.

Valentina told us how Emily loved to forage and take walks, "Nature Therapy," as Emily called it. She enjoyed nature and found peace with the outdoors. She had also stopped going to counseling. Emily dove into foraging after Joey died, being where she felt the best…outside. Matt and Emily loved canning, drying out different things they would forage, and she told us we would see the garage and where they worked with their collection of things they found.

Valentina told us we would learn about hangings. She told us to listen carefully later when Dr. Mc Daniel, who was hired by the state, would testify. He was not a medical examiner and would try to convince us that Matt killed her. His report sent to Westerville PD was what it took for them to arrest Matt.

The defense team would call on two to testify. Just as Valentina was about to retire from opening, she reminded us that there was no evidence and in Ohio a motive was not needed but an airtight case to convict.

CHAPTER 9
WITNESSES WITHOUT A CAUSE

The first one to take the stand for the Prosecution was Emily's sister who had come in from out of state. We wouldn't know then that we would be there for days as over twenty more would testify for the prosecuting team.

Audrey and Emily were just one day short of being a year apart. Emily was born on May 24th, and Audrey was born on May 25th, the year prior. So, they liked to say they were the same age for a day and Emily would call her sister on May 26th and kid her about being older again. That would be the last birthday they would share.

I listened to her testimony and the prosecutor kept asking her several questions to validate to us that they were close and stayed connected. They asked her if Emily ever talked about suicide. Prior to Emily's death, it was specified during the trial all the people close to her that had died. A close friend from AIDS, her first husband, a brother to her brother-in-law and her stepson, Joey all had died of suicide. Audrey and Emily's mom and dad had both passed away not far apart.

Audrey was asked about all these deaths and each time she admitted to asking Emily if she had thoughts of committing suicide. I noticed this and thought about why this would be asked or even a concern. She had described Emily as brave. I have dealt with death and my siblings or close family certainly wouldn't worry about me taking my life…unless there was reason to have this concern.

Emily was probably brave, but the poor girl had been through so much. Brave people commit suicide.

It was sad and obvious that Emily had many losses in her life. She was molested by a closely related relative for an extended period. Closely related and I will leave it at that. I wondered why the court on both sides didn't elaborate more on this. This to me could be a big reason for depression which could lead to many things for a victim.

She had begun counseling also after Joey died and had also stopped going. Audrey did not seem to be aware of the depression and wasn't aware Emily had been going to counseling. Maybe Emily hid her depression from her.

Audrey admitted her mom liked Matt and Audrey also thought Matt was a wonderful guy, but things changed during the beginning of the search. There were many searches going on, daily. She thought Matt should be looking for her. Later as days had gone by, Matt realized she wasn't coming home. He made a comment something like "I don't want to find her laying under a tree dead. Let the police officers handle it." That was the beginning of the end of their friendship.

On cross exam it was clarified that Audrey had not come home to search because it was toward the end of Covid, she wasn't working so money was tight and she had nowhere to stay even though she had a brother who lived about an hour away. She did help with a lot of social media. But Valentina got her to admit that she didn't search but certainly loved her sister. Audrey had reasons just as Matt had reason. I took that to mean one can't have selective bad judgement.

But I learned Matt did go on long hard searches. He had fliers made up and asked people to post them all over. He was met by crazies that accused him of killing her, screamed horrible things at him. He continued looking, posting, and followed a Facebook page for Emily.

He along with his half-brother and another dear friend from Vegas helped and they searched for days away from the woods. The other groups were looking for a body in the woods. Matt and his buddies had hope and were looking for Emily in other locations and had hope she was alive. They just chose to stay away from the group who were searching and making horrible accusations.

He didn't know trying to help and speaking down at the station would come back to hurt him. Westerville PD ran with that also. They implied he must be guilty or why wouldn't he continue to talk to them or search? Matt never stopped looking for Emily but after his interrogation, he felt no desire to associate with law enforcement. Remember an attorney also told him to stop talking anyway.

Sargent Williams was next on the stand. He was the first to speak to Matt and start the report on a missing person. Williams wore bodycam and we watched the bodycam from the minute Williams turned it on as he stepped out of his car at Hummingbird Lane. I thought he seemed very professional and was kind to Matt. I later learned he was promoted to a Sargent a month prior to the trial and was not a Sargent the first day he came to talk to Matt at the house.

He had questioned Matt well and asked intelligent questions until Valentina questioned him and she questioned him in such a way that she wanted the jurors to see that Williams was actually inexperienced.

He didn't ask questions that would be asked if someone was interviewing a possible killer. I wasn't sure what she was guiding us to see but he was the kindest police officer. Maybe he absolutely didn't believe Matt had done it until those conversations from others at the patrol station started. And wow, they started quickly. The next day on and for months, Matt would be under a microscope.

As I watched the bodycam, it appeared to me that Matt was immensely helpful. He was concerned but calm and he said several times that it was uncharacteristic for Emily to go anywhere without her phone even if she was walking but there were times when she left her phone at home.

She had left behind her purse, and her car was in the garage. I heard Matt ask Williams if he would like to look in the trunk. Matt just seemed to not be hiding anything but simply offering help. Williams noticed the bed was made and the prosecutors noticed Matt using the term, "her bed" and zoned in on the fact the bed was made.

Emily's clothes were there from the night before and Matt admitted he had no clue what shoes might be missing. The boots she had worn the night before, along with the skirt were there. I noticed the big, orderly walk-in closet as we watched the video, and I could easily see that it would be difficult to know exactly what shoes were missing. She had many and several shoe boxes above on a shelf and on the floor, all neatly lined up.

We would later learn Matt and Emily's clothes from that night before were there and Matt's in a hamper. There would be no blood, no fiber, nothing incriminating on the clothes, in the hamper, on the floor or anywhere in that house. Matt had a covid mask in his left chest pocket which was still there when the shirt was taken. But I am jumping ahead.

Rebecca, a good friend, and neighbor was the one that suggested Matt call the Westerville PD. The bodycam showed her as she arrived, walking up as Williams and Matt were talking in the front yard.

Matt was heard saying on the bodycam as Rebecca was walking toward them. "Oh, there she is, there's Emily," he said.

As Rebecca got closer, he then realized it was not Emily. Williams would recommend she go walk the area Emily was known to walk as he continued to talk to Matt. Later we would hear how many walked the walking trail and how much area was combed. No one went into the little wooded area that day. But Rebecca did walk around as Williams had suggested.

I noticed the resemblance of Rebecca and Emily. They were both small, thin and both had dark hair. It was spooky how much she looked like Emily. The prosecuting team rode hard with this. They thought it was an *act*. Matt was playing a part in setting himself up to look innocent.

A man in his 50's watching this small dark-haired woman approaching? I got it. My eyes are certainly not as crisp as they once were. I even thought for a minute as we watched it on the bodycam, that it was Emily, knowing that was a silly thought as I was reminded subconsciously, she was dead.

The prosecutors made a big deal about why Matt had waited until the evening of May 25th to call and why he didn't call sooner. It did not cross Matt's mind to call the Westerville PD that day because it did not even go through his mind that she was dead, or any criminal act had occurred. He also thought he had to wait 24 hours before calling and filing a missing person report.

He was SIMPLY curious about where she was and why she had not told him where she was going. But by that evening at about 6:00 PM when he had called and texted many people with no explanation from anyone, is when he decided he better call.

There was much talk that Matt was too calm, he didn't seem upset, he wasn't in a panic as Williams was taking notes and going room to room. Williams was making a timeline, and Matt went over everything he and Emily had done the night before. He couldn't think of the name of the water spring and immediately got his phone to show Williams the information which was readily available on his phone. All that information was confirmed. They were exactly at these various places.

Williams asked Matt if she had any medical history. Matt told him the name of the anxiety medication she was on but other than that, she was healthy. Matt didn't mention the possibility of suicide, but I thought maybe he had not taken his mind there for many reasons. Could she do this to him after what they had endured with Joey?

People commit suicide without rationale. But he still was not panicked and thought there was some explanation, and she would walk through the door. It did cross his mind that maybe she left, just left with some guy but that just didn't seem possible. They trusted one another.

"Her bed." Bed made. These two things Matt had said were suspicious to Westerville PD. He had not referred to it as *"our bed."* The defense commented about Emily living in the condominium before Matt had moved in. It was *"her"* condominium. *"Her bedroom."*

The bed was made. The house appeared spotless. The prosecutors made a big deal about this, too. I truly didn't give it much thought as we viewed the bodycam until they brought it up. I concluded, she was very neat, the house was *clean as a whistle*. She got up like she did every day and made her bed like she had every day. Habit and we are all our creatures of habit.

The bed being made was important. Had she come home with Matt? Had they really retired for the night together, both in bed together? I took notes to ponder that. It brought me to common sense in my own home. My husband and I do not sleep together. We are older, he snores, I get up a lot during the night to go to the bathroom. I have bad dreams; I talk in my sleep. We sleep better apart. He is an early riser. Most mornings I do not hear him get up to start his day. My husband has left in the morning, and I have gotten up to him gone. I don't panic. We have habits. We trust each other.

Matt and Emily had struggles and were dealing with many tragedies. But there was trust and Matt did get up almost nightly and go to Joey's bed, as he called it. He had told me she was particular and a little demanding. She didn't like to be awakened. He was polite and out of respect to her, he would go to the other room during the night to not disturb her.

I also sat there and thought about how his son had died less than a year prior and one would assume he struggled with sleep.

It came out in court numerous times, implying Matt drank too much. Emily and Matt both liked to drink and smoke marijuana. I suppose I might drink a lot or more if my son had just committed suicide. Maybe Emily was trying to shield some of her pain, too. There were never any reports of domestic violence in the home. Matt was a happy drunk and he went out of his way to keep peace in their home.

He would do anything Emily wanted to do to keep her happy.

On May 25th, the day she didn't come home, she had asked Matt to go to a picnic of a male friend she had just reconnected with. Matt didn't know the guy, but he was happy to do whatever she wanted. He had even texted her to ask where she was and if they were still going to the picnic. He waited for quite a while and wondered why she had not texted back.

It was shortly after he had found her phone in the bedroom. He got into her phone to figure out who this guy was so he could reach out to him to see if he had heard from her. He used her phone as a tool to contact many. He was on her Facebook and posted on her wall, asking if anyone had seen her. That also would be used against him implying he was on her phone to make it look like she was alive. Of course he had hoped she was alive.

It crossed my mind that someone might have snatched her up. She was small and human trafficking was everywhere. Did she commit suicide? Do people make their beds before they take their life? Did she make that bed, walk out the door not sure she would kill herself? Maybe she knew she was going to hang herself and she made her bed anyway. She was super neat and clean. Were the detectives even thinking of any of these possibilities?

All these things were going through my head, but I was waiting to hear more. I worked in EMS and retired from Delaware County EMS. I had responded to many suicides, seen lots, took care of many over the years. I needed more evidence to think Matt killed her. So far all I had seen on that bodycam was a guy trying to help.

I also watch a lot of crime television. I know these shows are fiction but many of them seem realistic. So, I kept wondering why the lead detective was in the courtroom sitting with the prosecution team listening to all the witnesses. If he was going to testify, shouldn't he not be permitted in?

CHAPTER 10
THE LAST WITNESSES OF DAY 1

Rebecca, Emily's friend took the stand, and I noticed it took her a few seconds to locate Matt when she was asked to point to him. I assumed she thought he looked vastly different. His beard was gone, clean shaven, minus casual t-shirt replaced with a nice dress shirt and short hair.

And wow, she did resemble Emily.

She was testifying on behalf of the prosecuting team. As I listened, she didn't say anything in my opinion to help the prosecuting team. It appeared to me that she was nervous but answered questions with not much information of concern. She looked like a classy woman, well-spoken and dressed nice.

Rebecca stated she liked Matt, they seemed happy, and Emily had been her friend for a couple of years. They had met at the pool in the condominium area, and it was an instant friendship. She recalled Matt thinking she was Emily when she had walked up to the yard the day Williams was taking the report. She agreed that Emily and her shared similarities in looks.

She had walked the bike trail with Emily on May 22nd. They went off the bike/walking path and into the grass so Emily could forage for plants. Emily seemed fine and Rebecca was asked by the defense team if she ever thought Emily was in an abusive relationship or needed help, would she certainly have acted on this? "Yes," she replied she would have offered help.

She was aware Emily was in sort of counseling, but she thought it had been required since she was on FMLA from her job.

After the walk, they returned to Emily and Matt's condominium and shared a few drinks. Matt popped out to say hello to Rebecca. The next morning the two girls texted briefly about small talk. May 24th, Rebecca texted Emily to wish her a happy birthday. It was much later, 6ish PM that Emily replied with some happy emojis. The defense team asked if this was unusual to only get emojis. Rebecca had said it was because Emily usually would type more.

My thought on that was she and Matt were out or heading home from their evening out and maybe Emily was just preoccupied. Haven't we all sent a quick emoji or a one-word answer on our phones when we are busy?

I watched Matt's face, looking at Rebecca, listening to her testify. He had a softness about him like he was happy to see her. I thought it appeared he genuinely thought of her as a friend. I suspected he worried as if someone had pressured her into making him look bad.

Again, I heard similar comments…Matt is a nice guy.

We retired for the day, and I was glad. Homeward bound I went to prepare for day two.

CHAPTER 11
KEY WITNESS FOR THE STATE- DAY 2

The judge was always so pleasant to us. Carol, who oversaw us jurors, was ever so kind, always going out of her way to keep us happy and comfortable. She was always swinging keys and smiling. She would escort us from A to B and send us back less traveled hallways to the court room. Media was always a concern.

I learned to just keep my head down at break time to leave the court room to go to the break area. I didn't make eye contact with anyone walking the halls and I didn't want any chance of someone saying anything. Sometimes just eye contact alone and a smile might invite trouble. I love people and always like to smile so I would be aware and remind myself to just ignore anyone walking toward me.

All of us jurors congregated each morning in the break room. We would head back to the same room during the trial. Many of us were coffee drinkers. We would make small talk, never speaking about the trial. I have decided to keep the other jurors' names out of my story because I don't know how they feel about this, and I wouldn't want to offend any of them.

I will say this, we all got along great, we had interesting conversation and each day we became more social toward one another. We shared stories about family, pictures, and our jobs. I liked them all. Carol always kept us in healthy snacks and some junk snacks. I loved that coffee pot.

Carol was wonderful and probably should be paid more. After all, a lot of tax dollars were blown on this trial. Many so-called experts took the stand and were paid outrageous amounts of money for their input. But I am jumping ahead again.

Next on the stand on morning number two was Beth, a dental office manager. She spoke at length about the office, her job, and the automated texting system for patients. We all are familiar with that. We get the appointment on our phone, a reminder, and sometimes can even pre-check in right from our phones. Technology.

Beth confirmed that Emily was a patient at their office and had a dentist appointment set for May 27th. There were copies of the messaging that we jurors saw. The office had even sent her a Happy Birthday greeting.

The prosecuting team summoned Beth for one reason and it was obvious as I sat there listening. They wanted us to think Emily certainly wouldn't plan a suicide if she had a dental appointment.

Valentina stood up and spoke for just a few minutes. One comment was withdrawn, and I was sure with her spunkiness she knew it would be but wanted to say it anyway. She said, "So we are to assume if someone is going to kill themselves, we are to assume they would call in to cancel their appointment."

As a juror I was supposed to strike that comment as deliberation, and I did because I had forgotten about it also. But as I recalled and refreshed, I remembered it.

The bartender, female named Kay was called to testify. Detective Loke had spoken to her and then she was subpoenaed in. She was one that had served Matt and Emily on May 24th. I did not learn anything from this witness. She served them, they tipped her, they didn't appear very intoxicated and were the only ones in the restaurant. Businesses had been slow since Covid.

Kay was able to visit with them since business was slow. She truly had nothing of importance in my opinion. So, as the day went on, I continued to wonder when the prosecuting team was going to give me some dirt. So far, a lot of wasted air and time.

The bodycam showed me that Matt was being helpful. I wanted someone to convince me he might have killed Emily.

Mallory. Now this was an interesting witness. They had met in college at Ohio State, bumped into one another occasionally. Time moved on and they had not spoken or connected in years.

They reconnected on Facebook when Emily saw a post about Mallory needing a car after wrecking hers. Emily immediately sent her a message on messenger which indicated to me they probably didn't have one another's phone numbers but were close friends according to Mallory in her testimony. I picked up on the fact they probably were not close friends, or they would have had each other's phone numbers. However, the friendship blossomed after Emily offered to help her financially.

Mallory moved around a lot, and after a brief time in California, came back to the Westerville area.

They were "connected at the hip," according to Mallory and then Matt was in the picture, and Emily and Matt married. Mallory didn't approve. It made me think of two best friends who do everything together and one begins a relationship, and the friend feels left out, and forgotten.

Matt and Emily invited her places, they partied and drank but she commented under oath that Matt drank. It appeared she was trying to make him look bad. They ALL drank. Once, under oath, she said they were not affectionate. Another time, she thought Matt was too *touchy-feely* toward Emily.

Under oath she said they had invited her to dinner at their place, which made me think Matt was trying to be social and accepting of Emily's friends. Once she stated she saw bruises on Emily, but I had no faith in any of her statements by this time. Shoot! I have bruises and don't know where or how I got them. Her last time talking to Emily had been an angry conversation because Emily didn't wish to listen to her disapproval of Matt.

She cried from the witness stand. I am sure having that argument and not seeing her again would hurt and/or make her regret her words.

I later learned in court that Emily had called her about Joey's death and Mallory did not attend the memorial service.

My take on this was that Matt included her in their lives and tried to friend her for Emily. She was a jealous girl that considered Emily more than what Emily needed from her.

Why the prosecuting team had her testify was mysterious and confusing. She served no purpose, and the defense certainly showed us that this witness was not creditable.

We are still on day two and I kept waiting for something solid, and tangible. The next witness, Linda, was another friend of Emily's. She came in from Michigan and this is what the prosecuting team brought to our attention so far:

1. Matt was too friendly.
2. Matt squeezed into the picture when she was trying to get images with just Emily.
3. He interrupted Emily when she talked.
4. He wouldn't let Linda sit next to Emily.
5. They ate watermelon.
6. Matt was drinking while they were all at the Comfest Festival.
7. Joey was pleasant.

We did learn that Emily and Linda had planned a trip to Hocking Hills. Linda said this was planned in advance and she said, "Emily wanted a break from Matt and Joey." It was to be a five-day trip but the morning after their first day there, Emily got a text from Matt that said, *Joey is gone, he is dead, he hung himself.*

Linda said Matt would not answer his phone after numerous tries. They headed back to Westerville. Emily was ever so upset, Linda said. Rightfully so.

Defense asked this defendant very few questions.

I have been to Hocking Hills several times; my son goes camping and four wheeling there. He has absolutely no phone service. He would periodically ride into town, just to check messages and text to let us all know he was fine. After all, four wheeling in those hills is dangerous and even as an adult, he is aware of my worry nature.

My service on my cell is splotchy when in that area. The cabins are in secluded, wooded, hilly areas. Again, this testimony meant nothing much to me and I was growing bored.

I started wondering when this day would end and the trial. It just dragged on like a boring black and white B movie. I started wondering when someone with any believable information would come on the stand. Show me he did something, make me at least wonder why he was here and help me to possibly see his guilt. and why we were even there. I realized this was a new experience for me, but it just seemed sketchy. And being a lifetime county resident and a retiree from the county with some knowledge of tax dollars wasteful habits, I was a little irked.

There were three prosecuting attorneys taking turns questioning the witnesses but only one on the defense. Oh, she had an assistant sitting in the middle between her and Matt, but these three prosecutors bantered on with nothing of value. Valentina was standing alone going head-to-head with these three and she truly didn't have to work too hard at this point. She had little to defend or discredit on the stand. So far. I heard a lot of opinions but nothing concrete.

We took a lunch break and most of us stayed in the break room assigned for only us. No one could enter except Carol, our keeper of the crew. I tried to read some of the other jurors' thoughts. I wondered if they were on the same wave link I was on. I was tired from all that sitting and small talk in the court room. I drank coffee and drank another and back to the grinding board we went.

A Jack Farmer was called. He was an older man, neighbor, who lived directly across the street from Matt and Emily's condominium. As I write this, I purposely refuse to call it just Emily's condominium. Matt came into this relationship with more money than Emily, but both were set for life. (I learned a lot after the trial.) I also learned how ignorant and cruel people can be on social media. I stopped reading it.

Jack seemed like a nosey neighbor. I thought his intentions were not to intentionally be a nosy neighbor. He sat in the garage and smoked cigarettes, one after the other. His father was nearly ninety and he lived there to help his dad. He probably had not much to do but people watch, as he smoked.

He didn't seem like a bad man, he actually cared for Emily and was a decent neighbor. They occasionally had a beer together. He often would do small favors for them, and Emily would water his flowers when he was away. Because Emily was a super energetic girl and loved to garden and do yard work, she was a bird's eye view for Jack, and he saw her outside almost daily.

He watched her comings and goings. He was aware of her walks daily and commented that she almost always wore black. I knew that was probably true because of the body-cam we had seen on day one and I did notice her closet full of black clothes.

Both sides asked him about Matt and Emily smoking and Jack said Emily vaped. (Vape cigarettes, known as E-cigarettes, have nicotine in them.) This info would play later into the case.

We heard several times how sociable and kind Emily was. She talked to Jack some and had met him a few years prior when her mom had bought the condominium. He mentioned Emily was moody and sometimes they wouldn't chat. He admitted to not knowing Matt as well. He heard a verbal fight one night not long before she came up missing. He could not hear what it was about and went on into his house.

The defense asked him in all the time they had been his neighbors, was that the only time he had heard an argument. "The answer was yes."

Defense also asked him if he had heard any arguing during the time she came up missing. He had not.

Jack took his dad and went to a cookout on Memorial Day, May 25, the day Emily was reported missing. As he arrived home that evening, he saw a police car in Emily and Matt's driveway. It concerned him so he went over to ask what was going on. Of course, he was upset and concerned about Emily missing. Matt assured him he thought Emily would show up and everything would be okay.

Jack was asked right away by Sargent Williams about the last time he had seen her. He said he had seen her the night before prior to dusk which would be not long after Emily and Matt had gotten home from their birthday night out. He also saw her that morning walking out of the house about 9-10 AM. I am sure Matt was relieved that day when Williams relayed that to him. He found hope in that important piece of information and the bodycam showed his emotions when he patted his heart.

If you want to see Matt's reaction, when his verdict was read, he patted his heart in the same way when Officer Williams had told him Jack, the neighbor, had seen her the morning of May 25. Watch it on YouTube. You cannot make this up! Matt would have to be an academy award winning actor to react in the same way months later. His heart had to have been racing on both accounts of extraordinary news.

By the next morning, Jack met with Detective Loke and his story swayed. He wasn't sure if it was that morning. We would also learn later that the bodycam information of Williams speaking to Jack outside was missing.

He also told how he recalled very soon after Emily was missing, Matt came over to his house and offered him money (extra) to go buy him a fifth of whiskey and a carton of cigarettes. Jack did it for him. I suspected from this that Matt was probably drinking with so much going on and didn't want to drive.

The thought went through my head...if my second child had just died, one from suicide just recently, and now my wife was missing and my neighbors were turning on me, yes, I think I would drink and smoke. Or was Jack making this up to make his testimony stronger?

Jack claimed when he took the delivery over to Matt, he smelled smoke in the house. From that day forward, Jack felt Emily wasn't coming home and he suspected Matt. "Emily kept her house spotless, and she would never permit smoking in the house," he said on the stand.

The defense team brought it to our attention and to Loke's that in all the bodycam, which viewed the house inside and out, there were no ashtrays anywhere.

Jack continued for months talking to Loke and said he had spoken to him by phone numerous times. Never once did Jack write a statement.

He was also in touch with Audrey, Emily's sister who was still in Virgina where she resided. Jack admitted to calling in license plate numbers for Loke when cars would pull in over at Matt and Emily's. He would report his findings to Audrey also.

He saw a party going on outside at Matt's one night. We were told by defense, it was family and Joey's friends, hanging out in in memory of Joey and it was his first birthday without him since his death.

Jack saw a car at Matt's for hours one evening and he was advised by the defense it was Joey's good friend who had come over to help Matt with google, maps, searches, information pertaining to Emily on the internet.

Jack had huge signs made and erected one on his front lawn. Matt attempted to go over and thank him for making the signs and was given the cold shoulder by Jack, according to the defense team. Jack did admit he had several reasons why he didn't want to reciprocate the hug from Matt.

The defense let us know that all the license plates Jack was calling in were that of family and friends to Matt and Matt's dad who was often there. Jack also couldn't recall many answers to questions presented to him by the defense. "I don't recall, I don't recall." He admitted on the stand that the mind is more forgetful as one ages.

As he retired from his testimony I wondered if there was bodycam used when Williams and Detective Loke talked to Jack. None had been presented on day two. I should have asked the judge that question since we had that privilege of turning in questions to be asked, but it was an afterthought and I pondered that often. I couldn't wait to hear what this detective had to say or if any would be produced since it wasn't on the bodycam we had watched.

CHAPTER 12
DOG GONE-DAY 2 CONTINUES

I learned the difference between coonhound dogs and cadaver dogs. Many, many questions were asked about the dogs that participated on three different days in k-9 searches for Emily.

A blood hound follows scent only of the items that are handed to them. A cadaver dog can use their sense of smell to locate human remains even in the ground or under water. They can pick up scents' minutes after a death or years later. One of the jurors asked if a body were carried and the body's arm would brush up against a tree or possibly in a trunk at one time, could the cadaver dog get a hit on that. The answer was yes.

Jeremy, a lieutenant of about 18 months with Westerville PD took the stand. He was not very tall and obese just as Williams was. The reason I mention this is because as a juror, I went down the hill, into the thicket, through the short woods. It was about one hundred feet from the sidewalk that ran parallel with County Line Road, a very congested 3 lane highway with a turn lane. There were no pull-offs for parking. I am overweight and much older. There were other jurors even older than me. It wasn't easy but not that difficult, as I mentioned for us to go into the woods.

Loke approached him on May 26th and asked to be assigned to this missing person case. Jeremy would oversee this investigation. This would be Loke's first ever investigation of a possible murder.

When the lieutenant spoke, he looked at us a lot, more so than any other who took the stand. I can't bore you with all the interrogation and the questioning that went on for over an hour or two as he was on the stand but this we learned:

1. May 26th, A search was done in the condominium, inside, outside, in every room. The lieutenant said under oath he didn't know if they searched the attic. Numerous detectives and police officers were inside searching. Matt was also asked to bring pictures of Emily to the Westerville PD which he did. He was then asked to draft a report and he did. Matt allowed them to go through his phone and Emily's.
2. Soon after the 26th or around that day, Westerville PD put out a press release with info on Emily, and a number to call, saying she was last seen on May 25th.
3. Searches began and went on for months by friends, neighbors, just anyone who wanted to help.
4. May 26th, Crawford County was called to provide a blood hound to do a search inside Matt and Emily's home, in the cars, around the perimeter of the condominium area, on the walking area, and by the woods. The dog was not sent to the woods where Emily was found. Nothing was located, no smells detected, no alerts.
5. The defense team mentioned that Matt had provided to them the wooded area, (walked it with one of the officers and pointed it out.) where Emily was found and told them to check it because she foraged there. The detectives never went down the little hill, through the thicket into the woods, as we did to see the location where she was found. Jeremy did not check it, nor did Loke and neither did a third detective as they all walked beside the woods on the sidewalk.

6. May 27th, another canine crew was called in from Cleveland, Ohio. This time it was a cadaver dog who searched the same paths the other dog had. Again, this dog did not enter the woods, but ponds and lakes were checked. No alerts at all again.
7. Sometime in May, Texas Equusearch was brought in to assist with searches and stayed for many days. The woods still not searched. Nothing found.
8. Equusearch was called and came back again in June also searching the Alum Creek area with nothing found again. They did not go into the woods where Emily was found.
9. June, bloodhounds were provided from Alabama. Same paths searched and nothing found. Again, the woods were not checked.
10. All dogs quit leading their dog handlers and stopped at the same driveway, opposite direction of the woods.
11. They did a knock and briefly talked to the residence at this house. They did not run any background on these people. (In defense of this lovely family, they obviously did nothing but my point being they were focused on Matt. I wondered why the neighbors weren't checked more to just be sure.
12. This lieutenant signed eighty pages of progress report, and he admitted he assumed his officers had checked the woods. They had not nor had he when he walked by the woods with two officers on May 26th. He said on the stand, "I wish we had gone into the woods."

They had hundreds of tips, had numerous call ins from people thinking they had spotted Emily. They said they checked them all out. They had not. Matt had gotten a text on his phone from some idiot attempting to pull off ransom for money and claimed he had Emily. Matt let the Westerville PD know about it and they asked to have his phone. Matt thought about it and decided he needed his phone, and he was sure it was a scam because of the poor English in the text.

Loke mentioned in court that Matt wouldn't give him his phone. However, Williams or Loke never followed up on that tip because he said Matt wouldn't give him his phone. The next day he did have Matt's phone but didn't look at this possible piece of evidence.

On September 16, 2020, in the woods that so many had walked by for four months, three friends who were purposely out looking for Emily, made the discovery. The lieutenant stated it was difficult to get down into the area where Emily was when the report came in. But the investigation began.

The chief-of-police did another public release and was stated saying, "We searched that wooded area three times and once with a cadaver dog." (That was not true, the dogs did not go into the woods.)

When the defense team brought this to our attention via to the lieutenant, he denied that exact comment was made. It was replayed for him in court so he could be refreshed.

The BCI was contacted, along with the coroner. Because Delaware County does not do autopsies, Emily's remains were sent to Dayton, Ohio after they had finished their reports at the scene. There were no suspicious prints on the ground anywhere near Emily. She was found in her typical running clothes in tennis shoes, below a branch with the USB cord around her neck, a vape cigarette beside her, a water bottle with a peachy color drink in it. It was tested and a 6.3% alcoholic drink was in the bottle.

That report was sent on to Ohio State, anthropology department. This entire process was completed by January 2021.

The prosecuting team sent it on to a Dr. McDaniel, a forensic/strangulation expert who concluded she had been choked to death. The defense team tore the "star witness" to shreds when the few they had took the stand, and concluded that Dr. McDaniel was not a pathologist, and not board certified in forensic pathology.

CHAPTER 13
ZERO EVIDENCE
DAY 3

Day three consisted of an all-day testimony from three detectives, Mellon, Blackberry, and Loke. This day went on and on. My brain felt fried, but I took many notes. I started to think the prosecuting team was trying to fill us up with an overabundance of senseless prattling. And I still wondered why Loke was sitting in on the entire trial prior to personally taking the stand. (I later learned he was given special consideration, and it was approved he could sit in through the trial.) Weird, simply weird to me.

My husband and I always tune in on Friday and Saturday nights to 48 hours, Dateline, true crime shows like this, and the police officers always interview suspects separately. So why was Loke allowed to listen to all the testimonies of his colleagues? This really bothered me.

Remembering that Emily came up missing in late May and by June they extracted info from Emily and Matt's phones. Matt provided passcodes to enter the phones. This was back when Matt was talking too much, thinking he was helping because that was his exact intention. He still had not suspected he needed an attorney but shortly after he realized they were trying to build a case against him. Matt had even given them a hairbrush with her hair fibers in it because they had asked for it.

Mellon's primary job was mobile forensics. The defense held up the copies of what had been taken off Matt and Emily cell phones. None of the detectives or the prosecuting team had printed it all out. It was every bit 700-800 pages, maybe more but was about 5 ½ inches in height when looking at the neatly stacked extraction in print. We found out that the prosecuting team who studied this from computers had 10-12 pages they used in court to try to show a rocky marriage, trouble, instability. Many months prior, the texts reflected a normal conversation from a loving couple. The prosecuting team chose to look at and dissect the last 6 months prior to Emily missing.

It was obvious to me that Matt and Emily were struggling since Joey had died. They both were just overburdened with grief. Some texts showed Matt telling Emily to give him time for the sadness to go away. "I don't want to argue," Matt said in several texts. He would tell her on some texts more than once, "Be positive, stay positive."

It was noted that Emily liked to argue in some texts. Matt tried to calm her.

March 2020, we all experienced the stay-at-home order due to Covid. The prosecuting team tried to convince us their marriage was falling apart. They weren't texting and stopped using the word "love." Defense threw it back, saying Emily was working from home. They were together in the condominium. They certainly wouldn't be texting.

In those 10-12 pages that were pulled, was there any text saying, *I want to kill you, I hate you, I want you dead, I want to divorce you?* The answer from Loke was and had to be, "No," because Valentina had combed through the texts, and she knew there wasn't. In fact, Matt had said in one, "If you want to divorce me, let me know." This made me think he was a non-aggressive personality and wanted to do whatever to please her.

Loke and his other detectives made a big deal out of the extraction from Matt's web history that he was looking at a murder in Vegas during the night after they had gone out. Defense threw it back at Loke that he had looked at many things and even the news. The death in Vegas was the same last name as his ex-wife.

What I found more interesting was that Emily's browser history showed a retail store web site she looked at for over an hour, which had a shirt that had writing on it. It said, *Into the woods I go, to lose my mind and find my soul.*

The prosecution of course did not bring that up, but the defense team was doing their homework and advised Loke of that while he sat there.

There was so much talk on social media that Matt didn't work, was living off Emily and had no money. The detectives implied this several times. They told us that shortly after Emily had gone missing, Matt had taken out of their joint checking account, $5000.00 twice implying he had paid someone to do horrible things.

Valentina showed us two bank accounts. One was Emily's which had over $97,000.00 in it. The other checking account was in both their names, showing a balance of almost $91,000.00. She also asked Loke if he was aware that Matt had inherited over $300, 000.00 from his mom's estate who had died prior to Joey dying. The two withdraws didn't seem sketchy to me after we heard more information.

One was to his half-brother, Paul who lived in Florda and one was to his good friend, who lived in Vegas. This sounded to me like a guy sharing his good fortune or giving them loans.

It was also brought to our attention by the defense team that Emily had a life insurance policy and Matt never submitted a claim to get the money out, even a year later.

We were told that Westerville PD went into the condominium with a search warrant within days of Matt reporting her missing. He was unaware they were coming to ransack his home. From the numerous pictures the Westerville Detectives took inside Matt and Emily's house, Valentina brought to our attention and to Loke to get him to agree that the skirt, black V-neck top, boots were the clothes she had on May 24th when she and Matt were out for her birthday.

Sitting outside the door in the garage which goes into the condominium, was a picture of Matt's shoes and Emily's boots where it was obvious, they had taken off before entering the house the evening of May 24th. Emily's socks were inside her boots. Loke admitted they did not take any of these shoes for testing.

Valentina continued to show images taken at the condominium and brought it to our attention as Loke was on the stand that Matt's shirt, Emily's V-neck were in the hamper in the bathroom. They had taken pictures with the clothes dumped on the floor. Loke admitted he did not test Matt's plaid shirt, Emily's shoes, or V-neck top.

White rugs and towels were on the floors in various places, and I noted they appeared spotless, no blood.

They took numerous items for testing though and nothing was found in the forensics report. No blood, no fiber of anything. The detective's activity log showed the cadaver dog was in the house for over 40 minutes with not anything to signal something of interest.

Something as simple as a greeting card with "Em" written on the envelope we viewed but Westerville didn't take the card or give it any positive thoughts. The defense team commented that it was Emily's birthday on May 24$^{th...}$

I picked up on this and assumed Matt had gotten her this card and it showed his caring nature. And life was good. They had money and were taking baby steps daily to be well mentally and physically.

Defense pointed out on the overhead, images of the kitchen, making note of several pink/peachy colored empty cans, an alcohol bubbly drink was on the counter. It was verbally noted, no ashtray anywhere. I interpreted that was brought up to discredit neighbor Jack who had said Matt was smoking in the house after she disappeared.

Defense also reminded Loke that the trash was taken, and nothing found of importance. He agreed this was true along with no vodka bottle found on the counter or in the trash. Matt had said during his first talk (which truly was an interrogation that he hadn't figured out yet) he didn't drink anymore on their return home May 24th because he was out of vodka. I took that to show he was being honest. It also showed that possibly neighbor Jack had not gone out to buy vodka and cigarettes for Matt.

It was brought to our attention that Emily had worn two necklaces, one longer with a layered look on their date, May 24th. Valentina showed the selfie image they had taken, and it was verified. I saw them. When her body was found, she had one necklace on. It was also brought to Loke's attention and ours as we listened, that Emily was found in a black shirt, but it was not the V-neck she had worn out the night before. She had tennis shoes on at the scene also. Totally different clothes were on her under the tree.

Her wedding ring was lying under her. Because there were so many comments made on social media that she was not wearing her rings, it was decided by experts that the rings were on her and as the body decomposed, they had fallen off. FYI, you media madness folks, she did have her rings on.

A vape cigarette was found in her pocket and another one lying at arm's length from her also, along with the water bottle which had alcohol in it. (As I mentioned before.) The vape cigarette in her pocket was not tested due to the obvious. It was on her as she decomposed, and nothing would show evidence.

Matt had voluntarily gone into the PD and let them swab his mouth to test the second vape cigarette and nothing showed of Matt's. In fact, Loke agreed on the stand that no physical or trace evidence was found on Emily's remains.

Valentina also reminded Loke that in his one year of eighty pages of the investigation, he never mentioned neighbor Jack even going out to buy these items for Matt. He also never looked at Matt's medical records at all. Loke, agreed again said, "That is correct."

Defense also said on May 27th, 2020, the GPS was put on Matt's car unknown to him. Two days after she had come up missing! We had heard this at opening, but I think her point was for us jurors to hear and think that Loke had jumped too soon in suspecting Matt.

There were a few hours that the prosecuting team drilled Matt about the timeline. We all knew the timeline from when they got home to when she might have left was especially important.

When he had gotten up during the night and had gone on into Joey's room as he and Emily had referred to it, he wasn't sure he saw Emily in bed. His defense was that it was wee hours during the night, dark, and I would certainly agree he would be confused or not notice. (I know I am when I get up during the night to go to the bathroom.)

The defense team asked Loke to tell her what time it was at that precise moment he was testifying, and he had the time wrong. Not too far off but she made her point.

The list went on and on and many things were taken for evidence but not one suspicious thing was found on anything taken and the house came up clean. Absolutely not one piece of evidence.

Things I noted:
1. Matt volunteered to go down to the Westerville PD and answered numerus questions for hours. He wrote down everything he recalled from their day/night out to when she disappeared, which he gave to them as requested. I listened to and watched as Matt wrote and he spoke his words aloud as he wrote, which made me think his report was facts and not going to waver, or something scratched out. He was also being videoed.
2. He removed his shirt and even pulled his hair back to show no marks of any kind on his body. Loke had

walked out of the interrogation room as Matt did this, but the other officer took note of it. All done without an attorney.
3. At the condominium, Williams had asked Matt for Emily's work laptop, and he couldn't find it. But he searched after they left, found it in the closet and immediately called them so they could get it.
4. He signed a consent to let them take Emily's phone and allowed them to look at his.
5. They wanted Matt's phone, and he voluntarily gave it to them and even offered his passcode into his phone. We live in a technological world and our phones have become a lifeline, but he was fine giving it to them. As mentioned before, he bought a new one and kept his same cell number.
6. He gave verbal consent for them to search the cars inside and out.
7. He offered the attic for a search.

The garage came up clean, but an orange extension cord became a big topic in court. This particular cord was always hung up. Emily was so neat, and everything had its place. Matt knew this about her and learned to always put things back where they belonged.

He noticed the orange cord, the same one Emily had attempted to hang herself with the day he found her, was not hanging in its place, and was laying atop the cooler. In noticing this and just possibly out of habit or just tinkering around as he waited on Williams to walk back in, he slid the cooler over, leaving the cord on the cooler. He felt it was important to let them know the cord had been moved from the wall.

What did they do? They tried to use this against Matt saying he was staging the scene to appear innocent. But Officer Williams on the first day as he took the report, he went inside and outside, leaving Matt, never asking him not to touch anything.

I noticed this and thought if she did kill herself, she had studied that particular cord, prior to walking out that morning as Matt slept.

A receipt from Home Depot was brought in for question. Valentina showed the image of a bag of Nature Care soil in the garage, which matched the receipt. Emily loved planting and working her garden beds. Okay! This seemed unalarming to me and of no importance.

The prosecuting and defense team battled back and forth for hours with Loke on the stand. Seemed he was to be another star witness for the prosecution, and he was being picked and prodded.

On May 27th Westerville PD came to Matt's in a marked cruiser with a warrant for Matt and asked him to come down to the police station to talk. They reassured him they just needed to talk. Although the warrant indicated suspiciousness, Matt was eager to go talk, thinking they had information on Emily. When he asked several times if they found out anything, they didn't answer but insisted he come in with them.

Instead of walking through the front door where the public can come in, they took him to a back door where several key cards were used to open doors. As Matt was sitting in the interrogation room, he said, "I didn't do anything, sir." Loke is heard saying it was odd that Matt said that implying guilt and covering for himself.

On that day he wrote a report as they had asked him to do, he spoke his words out loud as he wrote. This was brought up in trial and was implied he wasn't smart. My thought was he spoke aloud as he wrote to reiterate the facts and not forget important information. Those words were recorded and, on a document, and certainly could not be taken back or erased if he were trying to lie.

Valentina asked Loke, why it would seem odd for someone who hasn't been accused to ride in the back of a cruiser like a criminal and go in back doors and not then become nervous?

Loke thought it was a big deal that Matt used the word "gone" in reference to Emily. Well to me, as I thought about it, she was gone. Gone where? Gone how? Gone with someone? In court, Loke had used the word, gone, when talking about Emily also and that just showed me, gone could mean anything.

Valentina also went further in trying to discredit neighbor Jack who had said Emily never goes out without her phone. Something I thought was brilliant was Valentina had studied the extractions taken from both cell phones and the extractions showed steps taken daily on their phones. She told us all there are about 5280 steps in a mile. From the condominium to the bike path was about ¼ mile. When she said that I remembered dividing it a ¼ mile came out to 1320 steps. My tablet of notes was growing leaps and bounds.

It was noted that many days Emily went over two thousand steps and somedays only a one thousand and several days no steps were recorded. This information was big to me because it showed that Emily didn't always take her phone.

What was even more interesting is Matt's phone showed he was home May 24th at

6:53 PM until May 26th until 7:54 PM.

So, as I see it, Matt was home after their birthday outing, arriving home around dusk as he had said. He was home all morning, and the entire day Emily came up missing. He had talked to the police officers, talked to Rebecca who had come to him and didn't leave the house until May 26th.

As the hours went by, the defense team continued poking holes in the prosecution. Each time Stevens, the assistant prosecuting attorney spoke again to defend something that was said by Valentina, he said nothing of value.

It certainly looked like Matt was innocent. Westerville spent so much time with their tunnel vision trying to make a case and to put Matt away.

When I got home that evening, my husband had fixed dinner, and it was wonderful. I smelled coffee. That aroma is the best to me. I was hungry and I was mentally exhausted. I felt like I had walked over two thousand steps and I certainly had not, but my brain was full.

I heard a term more than once from Valentina, "Garbage in, garbage out." I knew I had to think and remove a lot of garbage.

CHAPTER 14
ANGELS WITH BURRS AND SCRATCHES-DAY 4

One after the other, the three women took the stand that had found Emily. They were two sisters and the other a mutual friend to the sisters. These women were the saving grace because they spent days looking for Emily and were the ones that finally found her in the evening of September 16th.

One had spoken to Audrey a lot to keep map areas checked off as so many areas were checked. She was one of the organizers who would inform others of the days and areas they had covered and mark off as others searched new locations. Various amounts of people would show up on each search.

She had also gone to Matt's initially to pick up fliers to pass out. Matt had put his phone number and Westerville PD's on these fliers.

Once the girls found the body, they called 911. They did not touch the body or disturb the area. Two of the girls stayed in the woods near the body while the other went up near the road waiting on Westerville PD. She did take the shorter route up being the same as we had taken, and the same area Matt had pointed out to the police officers' months earlier.

The way they entered the wooded areas, they found it full of briars, thickets and branches. All three girls admitted to getting some sort of scratches and burrs all over their pants.

The area where they started their search was further distance than coming in from County Line Road, the way we entered. Praise these three women for their persistence in finding Emily.

I could tell by their testimonies that it was frightening coming up on her remains, but they were ever so brave.

They all said the same things on the stand. Their descriptions of how they entered the woods, how Emily was found were all very well described.

The defense team didn't have much to say but emphasis was placed on the fact they had evidence on their clothes and bodies from their search.

By prosecuting team calling these three in to testify just gave me more doubt that Matt had not done it. I kept remembering how he voluntarily removed his shirt in the interrogation room and didn't have one mark on him. His clothes, the hamper in the condominium must not have had burrs on them or I am sure we would have heard about it. We also got to examine his shirt which was labeled in a bag for evidence. It was clean.

Our last to take the stand on this long day was a gentleman from the BCI, Bureau of Criminal Investigation, special agent Mick. His resume seemed impressive with a lot of investigations under his belt. He had investigated over one hundred crime scenes. The defense team corrected him on cross examination that technically it was not a crime scene but simply, "a scene," and his view going in was to be objective. He had to agree.

Many images of Emily were up for us to see again which were sad to see. I noticed Matt was purposely not looking at them. One image showed her right hand holding her ankle. The remains were in bad condition, but we got as much visual and explanation as we could.

We also saw images of the tree branch that had indentation from where the cord had hung for so long.

Much info was given to us on lengths from tree branch to the ground and from the branch to the top of Emily's neck. It was very graphic to see. Defense asked if he had gotten an image of the USB cord under her neck on the ground and he had not.

Defense had a USB cord similar in length and size and was very methodical in showing us and explaining how the cord was around Emily.

The body was placed in a body bag after the coroner gave the okay to do this. It was probably obvious that it was placed in the bag not intact due to the damage to poor Emily.

We would soon hear evidence for several days about all the places Emily's remains were sent for opinions, views, and professional opinions of many. Their degrees and titles behind their names were impressive. They all were highly educated, highly paid with county tax dollars and all motivated to represent their council to the best of their ability to convince us to go their way.

We ended the day, and I couldn't wait to head home. Again, my husband had dinner ready and again I was appreciative for that.

CHAPTER 15
ZOOM THAT-DAY 5

I could tell from the first two witnesses that this was going to turn into numerous experts giving an opinion on how Emily had died and what her remains showed on each of their reports. They came to impress the jury with their reports or try to confuse us.

The man who spoke first had been a detective for 27 years and then became a legal medical death expert. He became an investigator for the Delaware County Coroner. He was the one who had been to the scene where Emily had been found and returned several times after.

He had taken training as a master criminal investigator through OPOTA, Ohio Peace Officers Training Council. He had several certifications, one course in evidence.

He was also the one that helped and held onto Emily as the cord was cut and he helped put her in the body bag.

After her body went to Montgomery County, where the one and only autopsy was done, the remains were then sent on to Ohio State to be studied by a female who was a professor of human anatomy, biomedical engineer, and a forensic anthropologist. She had over thirty pages on her resume.

When her work began, the bones were hydrated with water and peroxide to remove whatever tissue was left on the bones. The purpose of this was for her to get a better view. The hyoid bone, the thyroid cartilage and the face were what was all in question. It was important to try to convince us she had four fractures that could not have happened in self-hanging.

She went into so much about the hyoid bone, which is in the front of the neck, below the jaw. There was much discussion about antemortem, perimortem and postmortem. There were some bones missing from one foot.

At times, I felt my eyes growing heavy. Thank goodness for the breaks and coffee. But they continued with each word and report dissected. I certainly was not going to get caught nodding off. Wow, that would be embarrassing. Quite frankly, I wanted and did give each testimony 100% attention. I saw many jurors taking notes, even the alternates. We asked many questions after each one was about to retire from the stand. I recall some I had asked also.

It was an awful thought, but my thoughts went into practicality mode. She had fallen no matter how or when, but she had partially fallen. Who could tell when these fractures had happened? I hated thinking about it, but I thought about animals, insects, weather, all possibly affecting the remains.

No one could rule out being savaged by creatures in the woods. No one could ever determine how long Emily had been in the woods. Not one expert.

Her body was not intact which was stated in court, and she had been moved several times from one facility to another. Her remains had gone miles from Delaware County to Montgomery County, then back to Ohio State which was another long distance. Then we heard some had returned to the scene months later and had found teeth that were tested and were Emily's.

It was also brought to our attention that several of the witnesses for the state had all spoken on a zoom call with Westerville PD, March of 2021, prior to all the tests. Reports came in from September 2020 to March of 2021. All were experts hired by the state.

The man who testified first didn't recall who all was on that zoom call until the defense read names reminding him. He agreed that he was on the call with several detectives from Westerville, along with Detective Loke.

Dr. McDaniel, was next on the stand that day to testify and was the one who determined she had died by strangulation. He was also on that zoom call. The defense team reminded us of all that the experts needed to always be objective. Without saying, I also felt all involved certainly had to be objective, including us.

I wonder how each would have reported their findings if they had not been on a zoom call, listening to others. It would have been interesting to hear their reports on manner of death without one shred of information.

On cross examination of both of these for The State, it was obvious the defense team had read every report and every line and asked many questions to contradict much in the reports. The Delaware Coroner was never on the scene but is the only one who can determine cause of death. His decision was made by reports that were given to him.

Valentina said, *"Garbage in, garbage out."*

CHAPTER 16
GARBAGE IN, GARBAGE OUT CONTINUES

I find it difficult to write all that happened on day five, but we didn't get home from this day until around 6:00 PM.

Accuracy for me in writing is important. I encourage watching the trial on Day five and six to hear the testimony from this day and you will hear so many hours of battling back and forth between the State and Defense. Go to YouTube on a rainy day and watch it.

We were thrown so many opinions, and experts, but Dr. McDaniel was an interesting man. I cannot begin to cover it all because you readers might get as bored as I did. But the Defense team livened it up when Valentina came out firing to weaken Dr. McDaniel's reports when his final report was that Emily was manually strangled. Like the few experts before him, their titles were long and the same conclusions. We heard that Dr. McDaniel was paid $300/hour and $3000.00 max for ten hours of work. If the female from Ohio State was paid that, double that in cost of just two for the prosecuting team. And remember there were so many more that had represented the State.

Dr. McDaniel has years of experience and is a police surgeon for Louisville, Kentucky Police Department, a Medical Director for training institute of strangulation prevention, and a clinical professor for emergency medicine at University of Louisville. He also worked for years in a trauma one hospital. His resume was eighty-three pages long front and back.

But he was not an anthropologist and not a forensic pathologist.

He was the first one to take the stand, turned his chair to face us the most and looked directly at us to answer most of the questions. When the defense started questioning him and would confront things, she felt was incorrect, he would smile at us as he answered.

He also had a skeleton structured *dummy* that showed the face, neck and he proceeded to demonstrate a USB cord and placement on Emily. The defense told him as she removed it from his witness box, it wasn't needed because Emily weighed ninety-eight pounds. Certainly, that *dummy* was in no comparison to her size, especially since she weighed about eighteen pounds when her remains were found. No one could validate if the cord had moved on her neck as days went by in the woods. In my opinion and logic, it would move as her neck became smaller.

There was never an image taken of the cord on the front of Emily's throat when the investigation was done so at best, images we saw, and the opinions of the experts were not easily believable to me.

He spoke a lot about complete and incomplete hangings. He stated that there was no literature or any studies showing an incomplete hanging like Emily's that would cause facial and neck fractures. Defense produced one from the Journal of Forensic Science and Medicine that did do a study on suicide and accidental hangings of 109 people and of those, there were some with fractures. (And in the age bracket Emily was when she died.)

He also didn't recall a zoom call with The Westerville PD detectives prior to Matt being arrested and admitted he never was on the scene where and when Emily was found. (He was on that call.) He had never met the Delaware County Coroner until the day before he testified.

All sides were given his report/findings prior to the trial to review. The defense noticed some of his report was taken from the OSU female's report and he also used her images for his report. His letterhead used along with his name, was his website which was not active.

He had to admit he read Westerville PD's report before his studies of this strangulation but wasn't aware or had nothing in his report about Neighbor Jack or when she was last seen. He didn't see any reports about what she was wearing the night before she disappeared and how she was found in walking clothes. The report he saw prior to his report was from Westerville PD.

None of his reports mentioned Emily's weight but in court he referred to her weight a lot. He had explained how heavier a person is that hangs themselves suspended, (complete hanging) the damage is worse. So, at 98 pounds, his theory of an incomplete hanging, the fractures would not be there from the hanging.

Defense also reminded him like the others, it should be referred to as 'a scene" and not a "crime scene."

I kept thinking about tunnel vision again. I am aware of that from years working and coming up on the scene of something. You cannot get tunnel vision, never. Not when someone's life is in your hands.

CHAPTER 17
COPY PASTE-DAY 6

This was really feeling like a job, getting up early every day and not slowly sipping coffee in the comfort of my home. No late-night Netflix for me. Being retired is sweet and I loved not having set times to be somewhere. I kept wondering how many more days we would be in court doing our civic duty. But I was also eager to get through the prosecutors' witnesses and move on to the defense team.

By the eighth day, I was impressed watching Valentina work and unless something big was going to unfold with the State, I wanted to move on.

Of all the days and times, we had to be there, including lunch, I never saw any juror come in late. We were all punctual and most of us would come 10-15 minutes early. We would drink coffee together, some drinking their tea. I always wondered if they looked at me at times, trying to figure out my thoughts on this experience. I sure was doing that, trying to get vibes from what they thought. What if we deadlocked or spent hours trying to reach a verdict? I had no idea what would be in store for me at deliberation which was coming.

Next on the stand was a very educated, well-spoken female that worked as a coroner for Montogomery County. She was a doctor, and forensics pathologist. She had studied a lot including in Italy and also a biochemistry and minor in psychology. She was middle-aged with about 15 years' experience as a doctor, and two as a forensics pathologist. She specialized in postmortem.

She seemed nervous taking the stand but there was something about her I liked. She did seem honest and just looked the part of a woman who did her job well. Isn't it crazy how we all try to read people but I did, each and everyone.

Once the remains were put in the body bag, she was the first professional to see Emily who was labeled at that time as "Jane Doe." She explained all the steps taken; numerous pictures taken before removing the clothes. On cross exam, she admitted she did not take pictures of the thyroid cartilage and there was not a fracture there. Her reason for not doing more on the thyroid cartilage was because it had tissue on it unlike the hyoid and she didn't wish to manipulate the area since it was going on to OSU.

When her clothes were removed, Emily's shoes were off her feet laying inside the body bag. On the images we saw of her under the tree, it appeared the shoes were on. I understood the reason for the shoes not being attached any longer.

X-rays were also done, and, in her report, she noted and said she found one fracture of the hyoid bone. She did not see four fractures as we had heard earlier. But she also had not removed what tissue was left and that was the reason it was decided by her and her team to send the remains on to OSU.

After her total examination, she waited 11 days to get the report back from OSU on their findings. She said she did rely on the report from them before she wrote her complete report. Defense again made it clear she had seen the exact info pasted from the OSU report also included into her report. She never consulted with the female from OSU after she removed the tissue to see if she might see things differently.

I did feel this expert was truly knowledgeable and did what she was asked to do and followed typical guidelines in relying on others reports.

But just when I thought I might hear something to sway me toward the State, this would be the third report, and both used the information from OSU along with their reports.

Next to the stand was the Delaware County Coroner. He has a full-time successful family practice in Delaware and came across very professional and intelligent. We learned that he doesn't go to all the scenes of deaths but has others who work for him.

One of his investigators went to the scene the day Emily was found. He was also on the zoom call with Westerville PD and the others. The coroner never did examine the body but did make a trip to OSU to speak to the team there.

Emily's medical record came up for debate. The coroner had studied them and did seem knowledgeable about what was in her medical and mental record.

In her medical record it cited she had Osteopenia, a form of Osteoporosis which causes bone thinning which in turn can lead to being more suspectable to fractures of the bones. Emily had past fractures of a severe ankle break and a broken rib or elbow. (I heard two testimonies, one saying her elbow, and another stated a rib) She began calcium treatment. We also heard earlier that she had broken an elbow.

The coroner felt with his knowledge, the low calcium issue was not severe enough to cause the fractures.

Her mental health record was discussed briefly, and it stated she had trouble sleeping, traumatized from Joey's death, worried, and became paranoid about Matt 's well-being. She suffered with guilt, had trouble focusing, experienced strange lucid dreams and was sad a lot.

Emily's record also showed later she was feeling better, clean eating, getting healthy and gardening.

She tried grief counseling briefly and quit going.

It was here we found out the water bottle at scene lying near Emily's left hand, did have alcohol in it. (I finally heard this because for days I had wondered what was in that bottle.) And to note from me, we heard Emily was left-handed.

All reports were incorporated, and he issued the death certificate. Cause of death he put homicide and manual strangulation. The true date of death could not be added since that wasn't known and sadly would never been known. So, the date he used was 9/10/20—other, meaning just that and using "other" is the procedure.

Matt was arrested June of 2021. The death certificate would not be filed until 9/16/21 which was a year later to the day Emily was found.

CHAPTER 18
THE PROSECUTION RESTS

As the coroner walked out, in came another female and it wasn't until the Defense called the first witness, I realized the prosecuting team had finished with witnesses. I remembered looking over at the juror next to me with a puzzled look but also relieved.

It occurred to me we might be reaching the end. Of course, at that time, we didn't know there would only be two taking the stand for the defense. No one else was needed I was thinking. But those two testified for hours.

The first witness called in from Iowa was cute, dressed very professionally and we listened for over an hour hearing about her education, credentials, and her experiences in all she had done in her career.

She held a PHD and received it from John Hopkins University and was a Certified Forensic Anthropologist for the State of Iowa and a professor of anatomy at Des Moines University. She specialized in the Laryngeal Structure of the human body. She reviewed many case reports and has submitted many reviews for the Journal of Forensic Science.

She held a position on the elected board of forensic anthropology. What impressed me the most is she taught coroners. That was huge to me.

There was much battling back and forth again about antemortem, perimortem and postmortem. We heard a lot about the hyoid again, the thyroid cartilage, and more about the greater horns of the hyoid.

I can name every bone in the human body with my medical background. This information was way over my head, but I did learn a lot as she gave me a visual using her own neck as she explained. It did help me to understand, and I found it interesting, too.

She came up with thirteen citations which meant she did not agree with many of the reports she read from the prior experts. One being, that she had never heard of soaking bones in a mixture of peroxide and water. She claimed that peroxide impacts and obstructs the bones. It bleaches them and, she noticed there was no time mentioned in how long the bones were submerged.

Matt had to look at images of Emily's bones again. That could not have been easy.

The prosecuting team drilled her, and her report was gone over and continued to be questioned on her expert findings. They did do a respectable job, but she stood firm on her beliefs that it is possible for someone to have the fractures like Emily had to be caused from an incomplete hanging.

There were many published, expert studies about fractures, ages of those that had hung, but nothing about a female of 100-110 pounds with these fractures but it could not be ruled out.

Gosh, there was even much discussion from all on width of ligature used affecting the damage on a victim's neck.

On one side bar, (which we could never hear because the audio was turned off during these) I watched the attorneys, and they were not happy with one another, and it appeared more heated discussions.

She was dismissed after five to six hours on the stand. She probably was glad to head back to Iowa.

We were dismissed for the day and would continue to day seven after a good night's sleep. And that was my plan. Eat, relax, sleep.

CHAPTER 19
RULE 29

I had never heard of the legal term, Rule 29 and would not know until after the trial ended that this occurred. I recall the judge telling us when he discharged us on day six that they had things to discuss.

I purposely went to watch this on YouTube after the trial and to also see one of the attorneys throw a temper tantrum at the judge and stomp out of the court room.

The mom in me would have been in his face and grounding him. Ha. But the judge was so even tempered and kind managed it with grace. That is all I will say about that.

A Rule 29 is when the defense can ask the judge for an acquittal if the evidence is insufficient. Defense told the judge there was nothing. No evidence, it should never had gone to a jury trial and ask, "Where is the intent to kill? Where is cause or intent of cause?"

She spoke on reminding the judge and Prosecuting team there were no witnesses to see anything, and no forensic evidence.

The State argued and came back reminding the judge of all the substantial evidence they had that could be what we jurors would see and would convict.

The judge was very patient and let them all battle back and forth on this. I noticed Matt's face as I watched the replay, probably praying from his soul to his toes hoping to get an acquittal.

I still could not believe how composed he was as he sat through all he had seen and heard prior to this. The State pointed at him and said some things that any innocent person would want to stand up and holler in defense and point back at them. But he held his composure.

The judge made his decision and said the trail would go on and the jury would decide his fate. We were not present for this decision when the attorneys and Matt were informed. I watched the YouTube video after the case was closed curious to Matt's reaction that the trial would go on. Matt's head dropped and his shoulders drooped. He had to be so beat up by all that had happened in his life. And now his future would lie in our hands.

If he could have known that day as the daylight hours were about to end and he was being sent back to a cold jail cell with no windows, we would find him not guilty. He needed to be strong a few more days and we would set him free.

CHAPTER 20
DAY 7-STARTING TO SEE DAYLIGHT

As we were about to go in to hear that last testimony, one of the jurors had gone into the court room prior to the day starting. I did not learn about this until after the trial ended because of course we could not discuss anything.

The prior day as we had left the court building, he was approached in the parking lot by some woman. A deputy sheriff saw it and told the woman to leave. I don't know what she had said to him, but he wanted the court to know this happened and reassure them he did not talk to her.

In came a very tall man who I will refer to as Ben. He was a professor at OSU of health biomechanical engineering, professor of health and rehab sciences, and director of research. He was also the founder and director of the injury biomechanics research center at OSU.

His resume consisted of forty-six pages.

His work involved much but also working with dummies in what I want to call reenacting situations and testing results. (These are my works and how I saw it and why he was called in.)

On October 26, 2020, he received an email from Detective Loke to see if he could evaluate the tree where Emily had been found. Simply put, could he test her equal weight hung and see if the tree would hold.

On November 11, 2020, he met Loke, and one of the other experts that had testified for the State and another detective at the scene as he was to begin this test. He had even called upon a tree expert because although he was an expert in biomechanics, he wasn't an expert on trees.

As I tried to describe this event below, I did it with respect to the experts and I did not go into detail, but I simplified it.

With him, he brought a camera to film and took still shots for the Static test. He also had an acquisition system which collected the data as he worked. Ben also brought something as simple as a milk crate, but it would be perfect for holding the weight as it was lifted. He also had a USB cord similar to the one found on Emily's neck.

He had measured the small tree that Emily was on, and it was one - two inches in circumference. The cable used was also placed in the grooves which were created from where Emily was on the tree. I can't imagine Emily's sister sitting through all this and hearing it, too.

Slowly he added weight to the milk crate until he reached 105-110 pounds and would lift record and take images of all. The test held and the branch did not break.

The Dynamic Test was next where he used a dummy that weighed equally to Emily's original weight and lifted it. He lifted it, dropping to give it the same energy from the gravity pulling on the dummy. The tree held.

He sent a six-page report to Loke and never heard back from him. What brought him in on this crucial day? The Defense team had heard about the test, and he was hired by them.

The State questioned him for quite some time, trying to discredit the test, I think. The last words that stuck in my head from the defense was, "The fact he had never done this kind of test before but did not take away from the Science and outcome."

AND......the defense rests.

Hallelujah!

CHAPTER 21
CLOSING ARGUMENT

Immediately after the last witness had left, we were read instructions by the judge. It meant we would hear the closing from both sides, and they would summarize their views of their side. We would then consider all evidence and begin our deliberation in private.

We could see any of the evidence which would be on our big table when we went into the juror room. They encouraged us to look through it.

By the time closing was over, it was late afternoon. They had each spoke for over an hour each.

The State reminded us that no one ever heard Emily say she was going to commit suicide.She didn't leave a note. To me that didn't prove anything.

"Got to love the bodycam," Prosecution said and went on about Williams telling Matt inside that Jack the neighbor had seen her that morning. The bodycam shows Matt patting his heart like he was relieved. He wanted us to see that as an act.

The State also wanted us to remember how Matt was staging, (acting) when Rebecca walked up, and he acted like it was Emily. I saw that as she did look like Emily from a distance, and he wasn't acting. The bodycam showed his reaction as he noticed it was Rebecca. Matt looked disappointed.

The bodycam showed me a guy trying to help find his wife. And I thought about the bodycam that didn't show Williams speaking to Neighbor Jack. The bodycam had helped me, too, but not in the way the State had hoped.

He wanted to remind us that Dr. McDaniel was the most qualified.

No, no, no, just no.

I remembered that the State on many occasions wanted us to believe Emily had disappeared sometime during the night of May 25th or that morning and was last seen by Matt. Well, no. She was last seen by Neighbor Jack on May 25th morning.

The Westerville PD had even spoken to the media and to neighbors saying she was last seen on May 25th, and their posters showed that. The video showed the prosecuting attorney and assistant on the news with the Westerville PD when that news alert was put out.

Most importantly, the State said at closing he had killed her in the woods on the 24th. What!! All through the trial, they had implied Matt had killed her in the condominium and dragged her to the woods.

Just hours after Matt had reported her missing, they spent so many hours searching the condominium. Matt had suggested they search the woods. Remember he had pointed it out to them, and they never chose to walk into that wooded area. They spent tons of money and time searching the perimeter and the dogs had stopped each time at the same house.

Now they want us to believe he killed her in the woods. Craziness. He sprang that on us at closing. This closing went on and on, as he stood at the podium talking the entire time. Then he sat down, and they were done. So, I thought. They had the privilege to cross exam after the closing of defense.

The Defense had worked so hard and had dug through so much discovery that was collected by the State. Rumor was there was 1000's. They had to find the holes. They found enough holes to make Westerville look like an earthquake had struck with a big magnitude.

Yes, absolutely the Defense were good. The best but it wasn't hard to see that Matt didn't do it. And at the Defense's closing, she went out with a bang.

She said many things and she sure did pace and spoke right in front of the prosecuting team at times and then right over in front of us. She first told us we had to prove reasonable doubt. Then she said something like this, "In my 24 years and 150 cases, I have never had an argument harder than this case because most times I have evidence to attack. This case is totally speculation."

She then went on about how the State had said minutes ago he had killed her at home and placed her in the woods and now their theory is he did it in the woods.

"That right there is reasonable doubt," she said. "Our justice system has to be better than this," she said.

I loved it when she said she is passionate but passionate with a purpose. I liked how she said she had done her homework and they had concealed records. She was the one who brought it out in court about the GPS Loke had put on Matt's car, and medical things about Emily.

For only the second time, I saw Matt cry when Valentina told why Matt didn't go look for Emily in the woods. "Joey had hung himself just months before. Why would he want to go into the woods!" (That was said in a raised voice.)

She reminded us about Audrey talking about Emily and her first husband being *two peas in a pod,* and how surprising that suicide was. "If suicide was so simple and you knew someone was thinking about doing it, by logic wouldn't suicide not exist?" (That was a good thing to ponder for me.)

She threw down on a desk, print outs of 100's of text messages between Matt and Emily but they took so few out to use against Matt in court.

"No one else would do it," Valentina said about Loke who made that comment. "No other suspect developed because they had tunnel vision."

"If mental health was simple, we would live in a better world," she said. "And don't all couples argue?"

She looked at us and said, "We had listened to so many testimonies and many of them would not recall a time or date, because it is easy to forget those details. Matt mixed up times after they read him his Miranda Rights and now, he is a murderer?"

The defense made a big deal about the orange extension cord in the garage and how he had moved it when Williams was there. They said Emily could not have reached it. (I later learned that Emily had a stool she used all over the house and garage.)

And as she was near closing, she said, "Emily had put a USB cord in her pocket so it would be hidden, and she looked normal in case anyone saw her as she walked out the door. Jack did see her that morning."

"Emily went to the woods to find her peace, and took the vape cigarettes, alcohol in a bottle, her vices."

There was much more she said but as I sat there when she finished, I couldn't wait for liberation and to finally find out how the other jurors felt.

And boom! The second attorney representing the prosecution team came up to continue. I wondered why our elected prosecuting attorney did not speak at opening or closing.

When he began talking, he stood closer to the jury box and repeated much of what was already said. One thing he said twice when referring to the trial and "the two weeks" we had listened...then he would go on.

We were not there two weeks; it was eight days and technically seven days and part of the eighth day.

But he put so much emphasis on words Matt used at the condominium when he spoke to Williams and in the interrogation room after he had been read his Miranda rights. I would be nervous, too, if I had my rights read to me just hours after my wife disappeared.

But yes, it did seem like the trial had gone on for two weeks. To Matt, it had been forever if you count the time, he spent in jail awaiting a trial.

He finally finished and sat down. I guess it was strategy for them in hopes we would go to deliberation and remember he was the last to speak. I thought to myself, if the other jurors thought like I had, we would remember but it would not be what they wanted from us.

In ending, the defense sold me. And the way Valentina paced and was dramatic through the trial, I knew she was passionate about winning. I was more interested in an innocent man not going to prison.

He got by with murder some implied after it was over. That was all over social media which I did read some comments again after the trial. Why did I do that again? It always pissed me off when I read so much crap. I knew we did an excellent job, and I knew we listened intently, and we had all the facts.

The judge went over some things with us and told us about the legal forms we would sign pertaining to our decision. He told us if we had any questions during our deliberation, we could send a message to Carol, and she would see that we got an answer.

He looked pleasantly at us with a smile and thanked us for our diligent work. He then excused the four alternate jurors and thanked them also.

Off we went.

Stay tuned.

CHAPTER 22
"UP TO BAT"

I am not sure I ever knew or had given it any thought, but I wasn't aware a red light would be turned on while we were in deliberation. That light would turn green when we had reached our verdict.

I didn't know then, but 1000's of people was watching the trial live, waiting to see that light turn green. Court TV was live through the trial and continued to be on until the verdict was read. I realize now how fascinated people are with trials.

It was late afternoon when we began our deliberation. We could finally talk, and I was ready to burst. I had so much that I had kept to myself and had not any ideas what their thoughts were or if they were still weighing both sides.

It was odd how we all just sat there quietly for a minute or so as if we all just had to breathe. Take a breath and exhale and begin. In the middle of the table was all the evidence that we were free to go through.

We had selected our foreperson. His duties were many, but we had no questions to take out for the courts to read for clarification. And he had no heated discussion from us to keep control of. He was the one that would answer the judge when he asked us if we had made a decision.

I was the first to speak as I was so curious about their thoughts. I kindly asked them if they were thinking as I was because I was certainly sure he was not guilty. I asked them all to share their thoughts. I was so excited when I saw all agree with me. It was the biggest relief to me and reiterated to me that my job in that court room was accurate.

I also appreciated the fact that we would not be a hung jury, and we wouldn't spend hours arguing or debating with a few to why they thought differently.

The only thing in the evidence we wanted to go over was the timeline because of the few hours Matt couldn't account for. One of the jurors went to the chalkboard and we broke it all down. We discussed it and no matter what some of the opinions were, it was no proof he killed Emily.

I remembered saying, "Oh for God's sake, he got up to pee, he struggled with sleep, he went into Joey's room and played on the internet hoping for sleep to come. And wow... yes, he went to sleep at wee hours. That makes so much sense to me because I struggle with sleep during the night. That doesn't make him a killer."

His smoking in the house was brought up because of the neighbor's statement and the theory the police officers and prosecution came up with. I said to the co-jurors something like, "If he did smoke in the house and if he was drinking, I think I would also if I had lost another child and now my wife was dead, and I was about to be arrested for her death."

Although some were not sure if she was killed by someone else, we knew there was not enough evidence to convict him. Zero was my thoughts and then we enjoyed talking about how no one ever took the stand to convince us different.

Technically we could have had the foreperson turn the light to green within just over two hours, but it was decided since it was now going into evening, we would go home, sleep on it and return the next morning to rehash it before giving our verdict.

As I drove home, I felt less stressed and happy. Happy the next day it would end, and happy Matt could walk out a free man.

CHAPTER 23
FLY FREE

We all returned the next morning as punctual as we had been all those days and returned to the deliberation room. I can't recall exactly how long we rediscussed our views, but no one had changed their minds or had any burning questions or doubts. It was no more than another 30 minutes.

Our foreperson walked over to the light to let them know we were ready, and I remembered he turned around with his hand on it and said, "Are you sure?"

We all gave him the green light, literally.

It seemed like forever for us to take our last walk into the jury box but then I realized they had people to call, and it took some time for all to return to the courthouse. Matt had to be driven in from the Sheriff Department. Good gosh, if he only knew that would be his last time riding in a police cruiser and treated like a criminal.

As long as I live, I will never forget watching his face when the judge read all three counts. He began to cry and all those days of being so composed in the trial and hearing such horrid accusations, he could truly feel happiness and a future. I saw him pat his heart and look over and I read his lips as he threw his hand up to thank us.

The judge stood, Matt stood along with his attorneys and the judge said something like, "From day one, everyone wanted justice for your wife, Emily. But the jury has said, justice for Emily is not injustice for you. You are free to go."

We were invited back into the deliberation room and got to talk to the judge, then the attorneys from both sides.

Of course, me, not having a shy bone in my body asked the judge if he agreed with our verdict and I will not quote exactly what he said because I had grown to like him and respect him but in part he said, "I am glad you found him not guilty." He also assured us Matt could never be sent back to trial for this. Over, the end.

The judge left the room and then the defense and prosecution team came in together. For those that know me so well would be shocked but proud of me for keeping my opinion to myself in what I wanted to say. My book can speak for itself.

They tried to break his spirit and wings, but this day would make him feel like he was soaring. And how ironic, the sky that day was ever so blue and the sun shining so brightly with the promise of a new day.

CHAPTER 24
I DID NOT KILL MY HUSBAND

Recently I had a morning and I started feeling like Matt. How innocent my morning was but so like a morning many of us have had.

I woke up in a quiet house and the TV wasn't on. My husband usually is up watching the news or sitting at the bar playing solitaire on his phone. He finishes his coffee every morning when I get up.

He is an early riser, much earlier than me. But I didn't think anything of it on this recent chilly morning. I did all the normal things I have done each morning. I got up, brushed my teeth, made my coffee, and checked my email. I scrolled around on Facebook as my coffee was being made.

A half hour had gone by, and I started to wonder where he was. I had just noticed his phone was lying at the bar. That was not unusual. I have told him many times when he has left, I wished he would take his phone. There have been times I have rang him repeatedly over and over and I hear it ringing in the house. We are not young anymore and we have kids and grandkids. Anything could happen, even something as simple as me wishing he had that darn phone on him to pick up some milk or Diet Coke on his way home.

I decided to walk out to the garage and noticed both our cars were there. Another twenty minutes passed, and I started worrying. My mind goes into dark places, and I also started thinking of Matt. How innocent this was and here I was looking for David, and thinking about the possibility that he had told me where he was going but I had forgotten.

Working in EMS all those years, I am very aware how spouses have found their loved one dead or collapsed lying unconscious. David has low blood sugar. Where the hell was he? I started to panic as I searched the house from one end to the other. I looked in the basement, in our shed, I opened his truck door to see if he was lying inside it.

I texted my daughter and my daughter-in- law. I threw them both into a panic. I have always been very levelheaded, calm, and rational. But I do worry more than most people from all I have witnessed in EMS. Accidents, illness, and death happen. That's why we have EMS.

I decided to get in my car and go down our road. He had talked about getting back to walking each morning and the weather was chilly but warmer than the past days. I found myself looking in the ditches. As I told my daughter, his OSU red sweatshirt was gone so I knew he had that on. Red would stand out as I looked down the road and rode around the high school that is near our home. And just like Matt, I knew the path David would have taken on his walks.

David has walked over to the neighbors or helped other neighbors in the past. We love our neighbors and we both head over for a visit from time to time.

Maybe he was asked to help one of them out. I hollered his name outside as I continued to look. I headed toward the woods behind our home.

Three of our neighbors work from home and I knew if he were visiting one, it would be the neighbor across the road. But it appeared he wasn't home. Katie had called me back, concerned and I felt bad worrying about her as she is trying to work. I truly have never had to call 911 but I was about to do just that.

I crossed the road; Katie was still on the phone with me. I tried the door on the neighbor's shop and immediately realized he was inside, or it would have been locked. As I opened it, I hollered David's name. He was there, just inside bullshitting with our neighbor. They laughed at me, and I was so relieved but so angry that he worried me so.

I remembered Katie was on the phone and she had heard the conversation. I put the phone to my ear, to tell her I was sorry, and her dad was alive and kicking. I called Lisa back who was about to come over to help with the search.

When he moseyed back home, I reiterated to him why I had been worried, and he just shook his head at me. I told him I felt like Matt and how innocent this was with a happy ending.

My point in adding this was because it brought me back to the trial and Matt. I didn't realize for a while David was not in the house. (Just like Matt had done.) Much time went by before I realized he wasn't in the house. (Just like Matt with Emily.) I looked over and saw David's phone. (Like Matt.) I started making calls. (Matt did, too.) I didn't panic at first. He had to be somewhere. (Like Matt.) I replayed in my head thinking I had forgotten something David told me, and he was where he had told me he would be, but I had forgotten. (Matt did that.)

I could compare the similarities, but my point is... if I had called the police officers, and my story would have had a tragic ending like Matt's, would I have looked uncaring because several hours had gone by before I called 911? Would I have been accused because I didn't hear my husband get up? Me being a female, the possibility and accusations would not be like Matt's.

This trial and Matt's ordeal will weigh heavy on my heart for a long time, as it has others. Matt? Imagine going through that and once being so happy and secure financially. How do the mind and heart find peace and solace again?

CHAPTER 25
REMORSE

I often wondered if Matt has PTSD. How could he not? There are many degrees of it. I have had a blessed life and something as simple as cutting my finger long ago as I was chopping cabbage, comes back to me each time I take that knife out of my knife holder.

I cut it to the bone and took myself to urgent care since my husband was out of town. I wasn't freaking out but knew it needed stitches. It is silly to even consider this PTSD, but it is a very mild form of it, I think.

After this horrid ordeal, Matt went back to where he was once happy.... Las Vegas. He couldn't wait to leave Westerville, Ohio and then once there he said he has kept to himself a lot.

When he sees police officers or cruisers, he gets stressed. He is aware there are good police officers, but the fear remains. His biggest issues are he trusts very few and has become paranoid often.

He sees people he knows or even those that don't know him and he wonders what they are thinking and if those that don't know him, recognize him from all the media coverage.

He lost some friends but has a great circle of them that never doubted his innocence but going through this has changed him. But though it all he is not negative and comes across optimistic. He finds joy in the little things.

A Westerville resident was listening to a podcast one day and the topic was about Emily Noble and Matt Moore. It perked her interest because she lived just minutes from where Matt and Emily had lived.

Stephanie remembered all the buzz in the neighborhood about talk of Matt killing his wife and how the media and Westerville PD had the residents in such an uproar. She had felt like most. He killed her, he needed to be sent to prison.

The coverage was so prejudiced and brutal in the assumption he had killed his wife. "They made us feel like Westerville was no longer a safe place to live," Stephanie said. "I think 90% of the residents believed he had done it."

Stephanie followed the reports, became very hyperaware and was happy when the bad guy was caught. "They sold us a story and I fell for it. They sensationalized it. Since the unfortunate deaths of two Westerville police officer in 2018, it seemed they wanted a chance to show our community they were tough on crime now and it motivated them to send a message."

Matt became the prey, and they acted fast. They took this situation and turned it into a way to send good PR to the residents. Open and close a case.

That podcast changed her opinion and emotionally upset her. Coincidentally it was about Matt Moore and his injustice. She realized she was wrong. Her heart ached for Matt and all he had gone though. She wondered why she had allowed the media to convince her Matt had killed Emily.

She shared the podcast with her family, and she felt she needed to reach out to Matt. "I guess I just needed to appease my soul," she said. Her family shared her feelings.

On October 25th, 2023, she connected with Matt on social media. She sent him a message that said: **I live in Westerville, and I want to say how DEEPLY sorry I am for how the news portrayed you in Emily's story. I am so glad that the**

real truth is being shared and our two daughters too-we all feel awful for having believed the things about you.

Just a few hours later, she received a message back from Matt: **Thank you for saying that. It is very kind of you.**

Since then. Stephanie spoke on the podcast, Alternate Corner on behalf of Matt and discussed her feelings and all that erupted in this sad situation. "My heart aches for him. Think about it... he is one person this happened to. How many others are out there," she said.

Ironically, Stephanie's work also involves working with the government. "Government work doesn't always work the way it should," Stephanie said. "I wish that people would remember that accused people are humans, too and to not believe everything they hear from the media."

And in ending she said, "Why are there no repercussions for the accusers who got this one WRONG?"

I will always wonder about that also.

EPILOGUE

Today, I am sure she took her own life. I was stopped unexpectedly going out of the court room by the media the day it ended, and I did make a statement. I was emotional and looking back, I should have just walked on, not saying anything to them.

CBS came to my home, and I spoke about it. I had some backfire because I said, "From day one, I knew he didn't do it." This was an example of how attorney's and police officers take one word and twist, turn, and make someone look bad. The public reacted and dissected my comment.

In clarifying that, I meant it appeared he was innocent from the bodycam I saw the day the police officers came to his home to take the report. He looked like a guy trying to help and offering much information to accommodate them.

But that did NOT mean I wasn't preparing to hear evidence that he possibly had killed her. I kept an open mind. Each day I waited to hear testimony that would convince me he had done it. I heard nothing day after day, after day. None.

I also implied at the end of my interview that "I hope they reopen the case and get it right this time."

Looking back on those comments, I truly felt someone could have killed her. I now know it was suicide and Emily just wanted her depression and sadness to end. I just knew Matt had not killed her and that was all we had to decide on.

Court TV had broadcasted the entire trial which I wasn't aware of until it was over. I wondered if those that were so outspoken on social media had heard the entire trial or popped online, uninformed and just to make the most ridiculous comments. Jumping to conclusion. I was so tired of people doing that.

Just in 2023, the National Registry of Exonerations has recorded over three thousand wrongful convictions in the United States. One out of twenty are wrongful convictions. Think about that. Imagine the ones in prison that have no decent representation and no money. How many attorneys jump to help someone who appears innocent but has no money? I suppose there are some dedicated attorneys out there that might take that case. But the more money one has, the harder they seem to work. They come out ahead in green backs but most times, the victim truly has little or no money left.

People should think about not passing judgement so quickly and police officers and lawyers need to work hard to get it right. Cops need to set goals in finding the right criminal and not looking just to close a case. Something is terribly wrong with these statistics. Who comes out ahead on these wrongful convictions? It sure is not the innocent victims that are arrested.

I personally could not sleep a night if I knew I ruined someone's life or took away years of freedom. I don't understand how people are okay with themselves knowing they almost destroyed someone. And shouldn't all these victims be compensated for these screw ups? I hope Matt can be paid for all this misery.

A few comments were made for instance, when I threw my hand up in the court room when Matt signaled a thank you to us with his hand up. Some took that to mean I knew him all along. See how ignorant people can be. Pertaining to Matt and the trial, social media is not worth my time and insults. As many said the absolute worst things, more people were behind Matt. How can his life ever be the same?

Matt published a book soon after his release. I suppose it was therapeutic. Maybe it helped his anger to settle. Certainly, one goal was to defend himself. For a guy who has never written a book, it is raw and real.

And just like social media, people can go on Amazon, write nasty comments about a book they didn't read. Read Matt's reviews on his book and see the *verified* comments and ignore the horde of comments made by cruel, uninformed people.

Matt also continues to do podcasts and not only to defend himself and to get his name back but to help others. There are so many in prison for crimes they did not commit. He has learned about so many things. Matt has spoken to families of those wrongfully serving time. They all have so much in common and can relate to each other's stories.

I have been invited to speak on some of his podcasts and I always do something to help him and to support Matt. Someone asked me why he keeps talking, and why doesn't he just walk away and move on? Well, his actions scream innocence and speak logically.

There are still those that think he did it and he just got off because the State could not prove it. They could not prove it because they had nothing. Some say he got off because he had such a great attorney. She was good but she didn't have much to prove other than ripping the State up.

Some said he had no character witnesses because he didn't have any friends. They didn't need his character witnesses because the State was so weak. Matt has many friends and an abundance that have stood behind him.

A guilty person that is found innocent, probably run as fast as they can. A man truly innocent who has had his name slandered and spent all his money to gain freedom, wants to be heard. He inspires and it helps him heal. He is defending his character. He truly never got to mourn Emily dying and express grief like a normal loss. He was too busy fighting for his own life.

I continue to have thoughts going through my head occasionally, as one witness after another stepped down after testifying. *Okay, why was that one on the stand? Did I learn anything? Why was that person even called in to testify? When am I going to hear some raw, truth about Matt possibly being a killer? Why did this even go to trial?*

It seemed they were just throwing mindless junk at us to see what would stick. What is that saying? *Throw a bunch of mud on the wall to see what sticks?* Were they just inundating us with so much to try to confuse us? Just think about it, they were all being paid vast amounts of money...our tax dollars at work. Matt growing poorer. But I wasn't confused. Their mud never stuck, not one bit of it.

Emily was deeply troubled about many things, she had so many issues with the sexual abuse she had been through and had kept that bottled up for years.

I think about how much Matt truly loved her. He had protected Emily even when they began questioning him. He didn't tell them right off that she might have killed herself. He knew it was possible, he had saved her once. And when he did finally share about her attempt once, when he was fighting for his life, it didn't do any good since his attorney said it was hearsay.

He and Emily had talked about how Joey was treated when he was taken away. It was horrible how they tried so many drugs on him with none that really helped. Most of all Matt did not want to believe she would do that to him after what they both had been though with Joey.

Many police officers, and the public thought he wasn't scared or panicked enough when she first disappeared.

As I sat there daily listening ever so intently because it was my job to get it right and I wanted to do just that. But I thought early on, even knowing she was dead and was found under a tree, that months had gone by and Matt's thoughts in the beginning were that she would just walk through the door. It made sense in Matt's mind. Emily had big moods swings, was easily mad and maybe was just upset and left.

There were many possibilities that I know Westerville PD didn't look at. For instance, we all know how sexual trafficking is so common and we all should think about how it could be in our own neighborhoods. She was small. Someone could have snatched her right up.

Maybe she sneaked off and was having an affair. Affairs are more common than spouse's murdering partners. She would not need her keys if someone picked her up. She didn't want her phone...if that was the situation.

Maybe she made a spontaneous decision, and a friend picked her up and she was just out. Anything was possible early on, but Westerville PD immediately thought Matt killed her. Of course, none of these were what happened but how did the detectives know this from the beginning when they had not followed any of those possibilities? She had died, they had that assumption right but that was it.

The incomplete hanging was important to understand and as I did decide in my heart she had chosen to die. I often have thought about how I wish she had left a note for Matt and his sister so there would not have been so much pain, such a delay in closure and hard feeling for some who believed he did it.

But no one knows what goes through the minds of those that choose to take their own lives. Statistics show many who commit suicide don't leave a note.

That day she walked away, maybe her thoughts were so erratic, she had no room in her head or heart to think of what she would put Matt through by choosing her own death. She had put him in her will, and she certainly would be sad to know he got nothing, and he didn't even get the condominium.

Emily also had in her will that she wished her body donated to science. When OSU was informed of this, they told Matt on a call they weren't interested in keeping her. After all her body had been transported to several places, studied for not the reason Emily wished. What flesh was left was bleached and scrubbed off her bones. Bones were missing. Matt asked them what exactly they wished him to get? He never called them back.

After all the crap he put up from people on social media, he finally got a chance to tell them what he wanted. A group of supporters were constantly posting on Emily's Facebook wall. One announced that Emily's remains were left to OSU for science.

Matt went on Emily's Facebook and posted what really happened to her remains. **OSU didn't want them, and Emily could care less about OSU. She would have sent her remains elsewhere if she would have had the opportunity.**

He proceeded and posted to these people they did not personally know Emily, **to get a life.**

Just so many unfortunate things for Emily and Matt. Maybe if Westerville PD would have zoned in on any and every possibility, she would have been found sooner and it would have been easier to determine the cause of death. The family would have had closure much sooner. I wouldn't have had the opportunity to write about it. I prefer to write humor. There would not have been a grand jury trial. Matt's inheritance from his mom would have been to live comfortably and certainly not to be spewed away to gain freedom for a crime he didn't commit.

But hard feelings, bad press, wasted tax dollars, breaking Matt financially and taking every cent he had and putting an innocent man behind bars for over a year was tragic. Going to trial should not have happened.

Then just has life settled, I got a call from 48 Hours and Dateline. It ended up being Dateline who wrote the story and aired it in the fall of 2023.

Delaware County was great about keeping the jurors' contact info private as much as possible. I am not sure how many jurors responded, interested in speaking to Dateline but I opted to speak to them along with two other females.

I had several email correspondences from a female. I think she was the editor, but I can't quite remember her exact title. It seemed she wore many hats in the operation of it.

As far as dress, she recommended anything we wished but to not wear something busy in color or in solid white. We were to bring our makeup in case she wanted to do any touch ups. She touched up the other two girls' makeup but said mine was perfect. Ha! It amazes my family to how fast I put on my makeup, be ready to head out the door. My after thought was maybe she just thought my old skin was hopeless.

They met us on a scheduled day in Columbus at The Valley Dale Ballroom, the coolest old Music Hall where musician played back in the Big Ban era in the 1930's and 1940's. It began as a stagecoach stop in the 1880's and talking to the owner and hearing so many cool stories made my trip worth the morning drive. The time we gave Dateline, not so much.

When Dennis Murphy walked in, I was excited to meet him and what a nice man. It was amazing all the equipment and crew that came in to make this happen. Imagine how many places they travel just to put a show together.

They spoke to us with a camera and lights on us for several hours. When the Dateline episode aired, it was disappointing how little they aired from our comments. I thought our comments were valid and good. Airtime was given to some that truly didn't deserve it.

They had also talked to me off camera to give me time to think about my comment made on the news when I said," I knew he was innocent from day one." I absolutely wanted to answer that, and they could have asked me spontaneously on the air. Do you know they didn't air that also?

They probably must watch what is aired so they look unbiased so maybe they edited out the majority of our comments. They needed to add controversial comments to keep the viewers wondering.

I remember kidding the camera guy about filming from the waist up which totally pissed me off when the little that aired showed was full body. Ugh to that but that was not the reason I had gone.

During the filming, the editor asked us if we had ever seen the one part of the interrogation that had not made it to court and if we would like to see it? I supposed it might be on the internet somewhere, but I was curious. She walked over, played it from her laptop. If they were filming us as we watched it, which did not get airtime, I think it would have shown our raw, real reactions. Mine was shocking.

I have watched a lot of police shows, but this was real. The footage was less than a week after Emily had been missing. It was appalling what I watched. Detectives were in Matt's face, screaming to him that he did it, he killed Emily. Saying things like, "Admit it, you did it. You killed her." Then as Matt spoke on, they took things from that to try to use against him, after he was so shaken up by their angry accusations. I guess that is what a scary tactic is, but Matt didn't break.

It felt like several bullies on a playground with a kid backed into the playground fence, screaming into his face. They were obviously trying to break him. He said over and over and over, "I did not kill Emily, I did not kill my wife."

When I watched this, it reminded me of cases and how someone admits to killing someone and then recants. Under pressure for hours, I can truly now see how someone could break. But Matt always said he did not do it. They couldn't break him down.

Unfortunately for what reason, this was not put on the episode for all to see. And it was never played in court.

I just wanted my views of this case aired. Ater all, it was on during prime time for viewers to see. The timing of our interviews was not long after the trial and I was still angry and disappointed in the courts and Westerville Patrol Department and the turmoil they had put Matt through.

I felt and continue to feel it is not okay to take a person's money, leave him poor and be wrong in an arrest and just get to walk away and sleep at night. Financial security goes on for some, many getting richer and with no consequences. Imagine how many innocent people are in prison because they didn't have the money to prove their innocence. Matt's is gone but as he says," I have my freedom and maybe this all happened for a reason."

And he is out telling his story. He is rightfully so...mad.

Matt was satisfied with the episode when it aired and felt they certainly did not make him look like the monster so many portrayed him as. Compared to others who promised to tell his story and to give him hope, and just took his money with absolutely no help but stirring more public, false information. So, I supposed he was happy since Dateline did allow him much airtime and treated him with the due respect that was a long time coming.

I do think if many of the staff from Dateline were asked and could speak freely, they would agree he was wronged.

Matt got his airtime and that made it okay even if our time was wasted.

He has learned to live on and just give up on those that chose to remove him from their lives. It saddens me also how so many who weren't involved, didn't hear the case, and make uneducated comments about him. Some still believe he did it. We jurors did an excellent job.

We gave him his life back and to have that kind of power to fix a wrong is total bliss. And he got to eat that steak with his stepmom the day he walked out a free man.

www.ingramcontent.com/pod-product-compliance
Lightning Source LLC
LaVergne TN
LVHW041709060526
838201LV00043B/649

In September 2020, the body of Emily Noble was recovered from a wooded area in Westerville, Ohio, near her home. She had been missing for months when volunteers found her body. What appeared to be a suicide, law enforcement directed their attention on Matheau Moore, and he was arrested for the murder of his wife.

Connie was a juror of Matheau's trial, and the things she saw in the courtroom have stayed with her long after the verdict.

Matheau Moore was wrongfully accused in killing his wife and served almost two years in jail awaiting a trial. He is forced to spend his entire inheritance. Through the eyes of a juror, readers will follow each day in the court room and see how Moore finally gets what he deserves—his freedom.

In Juror Number 8, readers will follow the true story of how Matheau Moore's accusation become a high-profile case featured on Court TV, Dateline, and more. Social media opinions unfold in outrage.

Connie hopes to impart on readers that there can be flaws in the judicial system and police departments. Not all sent to prison are guilty, and some of the most misfortunate are wrongfully accused and fail to receive proper representation due to lack of funds. Most of all, Connie hopes readers also see Matheau's innocence and that the jurors, in fact, got it right: Matheau Moore deserves his respected name back.

ABOUT THE AUTHOR

A Delaware, Ohio native, Connie Curry has crafted humor into writing, inspired by her daily life. She was a columnist for her local paper and wrote her first book, GIVE ME BACK MY GLORY after a breast cancer diagnosis.

Her humor has graced various magazines and won awards. Connie received the top award in the James Thurber Annual Humor Contest; also, her short story "HOMEWORK ASSIGNMENT" was featured in I WANNA BE SEDATED and NOT YOUR MOTHER'S BOOK on SEX.

After retiring from EMS, Connie and her husband spend their time also at their Lake Erie tiny house and Tennessee cabin. They are blessed with three children and six grandchildren.

PALMETTO
PUBLISHING
Charleston, SC
www.PalmettoPublishing.com

ISBN 979-8-8229-6139-5